Ocean

Ocean

An Introduction to
Jodo-Shinshu Buddhism
in America

A Dialogue
with Buddhists & Others

Kenneth K. Tanaka

WisdomOcean Publications
Berkeley, California

LIBRARY OF CONGRESS CATALOGING-IN-PUBLICATION DATA

Tanaka, Kenneth Kenichi 1947-
 Ocean: An Introduction to Jodo-Shinshu Buddhism in America
 Includes bibliographical references and index
 1. Jodo-Shinshu Buddhism. 2. Buddhist sect. 3. Buddhism-
Relations-Christianity 4. Religions in America 5. Spiritual life -
Comparative studies

Library of Congress Catalog Card Number: 97-90710
ISBN 0-9658062-0-0

AVAILABLE FROM:

The Buddhist Bookstore
Buddhist Churches of America
1710 Octavia Street
San Francisco, California 94109
Tel. (415)776-7877, Fax (415) 771-6293

Honpa Hongwanji Mission of Hawaii Headquarters Bookstore
1727 Pali Highway
Honolulu, Hawaii 96813
Tel. (808) 522-9200, Fax (808) 522-9209

Bookstore of the Buddhist Churches of Canada
11786 Fentiman Place
Richmond, B.C. V7E 3M4 Canada
Tel. (604) 272-3330, Fax (604) 272-6865

WisdomOcean Publications
P.O. Box 7885
Berkeley, California 94707-0885
Fax (510) 525-7912, Email: WisOcean@aol.com

To my wife Kimie

Table of Contents

i

Table of Contents

Ocean

Preface

It has been a dream for some time to publish an introductory level book on Jodo-Shinshu (or Shin, Shinshu or Pure Land School), one of the largest Buddhist schools with a one-hundred-year-old history in North America. I first began writing this for Jodo-Shinshu Buddhists, but as the project evolved I felt compelled to make it accessible to a wider readership.

I have kept explanations simple, concise, direct, and readable for everyone, including high school students. The question and answer format stems from my initial goal of offering a set of guidelines for Jodo-Shinshu Buddhists when responding to questions by non-Buddhists. This need continues to challenge Jodo-Shinshu Buddhists. Because of this format, the language takes on an informal and colloquial character. The questions are intended to reflect many of the frequently asked questions. (For a list of main questions, see Index A.) The interlocuter can be anyone the reader wishes to imagine as his or her partner.

From the outset, I wish to state that I have a great respect for the Western religions. I intend neither criticism nor negative portrayal of any faith. I do not intend for readers to take my evaluations of Buddhism as an automatic criticism of other religions. This is not a see-saw, where an elevation of one religion equals a put-down of another.

Dialogue with people from other faiths has always reaffirmed my respect and esteem for their traditions. I strongly believe in the importance of interfaith dialogue, which I have supported in my professional career through teaching dialogue courses with Christianity and Judaism. Our increasingly pluralistic communities demand mutual understanding and transformation for our survival. As an American Buddhist, I hope my fellow North Americans will embrace a greater understanding for a tradition that, despite its shorter history on this continent, is now part of the religious fabric of this nation.

The content is an expression of my personal understanding and appreciation of the Jodo-Shinshu Buddhist tradition, and does not claim to represent any institution or its official doctrinal position. I have tried to live up to the long-held practice of being faithful to the tradition (*dento*) while putting forth my own appreciation (*kosho*). This project has, if anything, helped me to clarify my own understanding. I hope that readers will find it fruitful.

Preface

I owe much to numerous individuals who provided encouragement along the way. I am deeply grateful to the following persons for their valuable suggestions through the early drafts: Diane Ames, Barry Barankin, Stephen Browning, Anne Carlson, Kelsi Cell, Pastor Hajime Fujii, Karen Fujii, Steven Gasner, Walter Hashimoto, Ann Ishikawa, Ken Kaji, Andrew Kobayashi, Anastasia McGhee, Debbie Malone, Mary Ann Miyao, Brian Nagata, Paul Nagy, Kiyo Inada, Margie Oishi, Dale Schellenger, Catherine Shaw, Calvin Steimetz, Edward Thompson, Clifford Tokumaru, John Wardell and Margaret Yam. It is always reassuring to receive support and professional input from Jodo-Shinshu priests. I cherish the efforts made by Reverends Don Castro, Russell Hamada, Ron Kobata, Harold Oda, Kanya Okamoto, and Dennis Shinseki.

I am especially indebted to Sharon Winters for her careful editorial suggestions and to Barbara Harrison for the arduous task of typing the original draft. To Dr. Roy Mayhugh, words are insufficient to adequately convey my deep appreciation for his enthusiastic and professional support in the editing of the text. I wish to express my appreciation to Rev. Bob Oshita and the approximately eighty members of the study class of the Sacramento Betsuin Buddhist Church who embraced my book project with enthusiasm, constructive criticism and true caring.

The support for the publication of this book has been enormous. The book is endorsed by the following organizations affiliated with the Buddhist Churches of America: Bay District Ministers' Association, Bay District

Buddhist Education Committee, and the Buddhist Education Committee of the Southern Alameda County Buddhist Church. I am, further, pleased that this book is included among the projects supported by the Propagation and Research Committee of the B.C.A. Ministers' Association.

Finally, this project could not have been realized without the generous funding from the Sunao Kikunaga Scholarship, the Sudhana Memorial Fund, the Federation of Dharma School Teachers' League and the Rev. G. Kono Memorial Scholarship Fund. I am indebted to the donors of the Rev. Yoshitaka Tamai Professorial Chair, the members of the Southern Alameda County Buddhist Church, and the Institute of Buddhist Studies for the professional positions that afforded me the opportunity to complete this book.

Abbreviations and Conventions

B.C.E.   Before the Common Era = B.C.

ca.   *circa*; about; around.

C.E.   Common Era = A.D.

Letters   *Letters of Shinran* (Mattosho).
          Kyoto: Hongwanji International Center,
          1978

Pure Land Inagaki, Hisao. *The Three Pure Land Sutras.*
          Kyoto: Nagata Bunshodo, 1994.

Tannisho   Unno, Taitetsu, trans.
          Tannisho: A Shin Buddhist Classic.
          Honolulu: Buddhist Study Center Press,
          1984.

Teachings *The True Teachings, Practice and Realizatio*
          of the Pure Land Way (Kyogyoshinsho).
          Volumes I–IV Kyoto: Hongwanji
          International Center, 1983-90.

Ocean

Introduction

Ocean Parable

I remember a Dharma talk (Buddhist sermon) story about a sailor lost at sea. I can't recall the name of the priest who gave the talk. I would like to give him proper credit for the story. Maybe it is in the nature of religious development that we are nurtured more by our unconscious impressions than by our clear memories.[1]

I have expanded the story a little so that I can use it to capture the heart of Jodo-Shinshu Buddhism—its doctrine and spirituality. Here is the story, an ocean metaphor.

At night a ship leaves the port of a tropical island. After many hours on the high seas a sailor falls overboard. No

---

1 More recently others have written about this metaphor, for example, Dr. Alfred Bloom, Rev. Masao Kodani and Rev. Tetsuo Unno.

one on the ship notices that the man is missing, and the ship sails on its way. The water is chilly, and the waves are choppy. It is hauntingly dark. The sailor paddles frantically to keep afloat.

He then starts to swim toward an island he saw before he fell overboard. He has lost all sense of direction. So he is not sure that he is heading the right way. Though he is a good swimmer, his arms and legs soon grow weary. His lungs are tired, and he gasps for air. The sailor feels lost and totally alone in the middle of the ocean. This could be the end for him. As despair overcomes him, his energy drains from him like sand from an hourglass. He begins to choke on the water slapping his face, and he can feel his body being dragged under.

At this instant he hears a voice from the depths of the ocean, "Let go. Let go of your striving! You're fine just as you are! Namo Amida Butsu."

The sailor hears the voice and stops his useless striving to swim by his own power. Instead, he turns over on his back with limbs outstretched as if he were in a backyard hammock on a lazy summer afternoon. He is overjoyed to find that the ocean holds him afloat without any effort on his part!

Now, the water feels warm and the waves are calm. The ocean that seemed ready to drag him under now caresses him. He is grateful and happy to know that he is all right. He realizes that he was fine all along. He just didn't know it. The ocean has not changed at all. By changing his thinking, the sailor's relationship with the ocean has changed. The sea changed from being a dangerous and frightening enemy to a friend who embraced and supported him.

The sailor knows that he cannot stay afloat forever in the middle of the ocean. If he had no worldly obligations, maybe he could afford to stay and rest in this joyful calm. But the image of his wife and small children waiting anxiously at home inspires him to try to reach the shore.

He begins to swim as before, but with one important difference. He now trusts the ocean as he would a caring and protecting loved one. He knows that whenever he becomes tired, he can let go, and the ocean will support him. More importantly, he now knows that while he swims, it is the power of the ocean, not his own power that keeps him afloat. Yes, he moves his limbs to swim, but he has learned he can stay afloat by not striving.

Now that he feels safe in the arms of the sea, the sailor can think about finding the island. He studies the positions of the stars and the moon and the direction of the wind. Using his training as a sailor, he imagines where the island might be and moves toward it. The swimmer has no guarantee that he has chosen the right direction, but he is now sure that the ocean will not let him drown. Eventually he will reach the island. In appreciation for this newfound confidence and joy, the sailor hears himself uttering, "Namo Amida Butsu."

This story, in a nutshell, captures the heart of Jodo-Shinshu spirituality. The drowning sailor symbolizes our human condition which is best explained by the Buddha's realization, "We all experience suffering." Our natural response is to attempt to swim out of our predicament.

But no matter how strong and well-trained, we are unable to swim to the distant island. Try as we might, the effort is futile. At that very point, we are called to let go of our struggle and to trust the ocean. The result is a dramatic change, in which we experience release, joy and awareness. Within this Jodo-Shinshu spiritual transformation called "Shinjin awareness," we are infused with an abiding sense of well-being and a spontaneous desire to assist others to reach happiness.

Shinran Shonin (1173–1263), the founder of the Jodo-Shinshu school, was extremely fond of the ocean imagery. He refers to the ocean in speaking about his own unenlightened, desperate predicament. He laments:

> I know truly how grievous it is that I, Gutoku Shinran, am sinking in an immense ocean of desires and attachment and am lost in vast mountains of fame and advantage.
>
> (*Teachings*, II, p. 279)

The same ocean imagery, however, expresses the joyous and liberating dimensions of his spiritual life. He speaks of the "Ocean-like Primal Vow" and "Sea of Inconceivable Virtue." Elsewhere, he exclaims:

> How joyous I am, my heart and mind being rooted in the Buddha-ground of the universal Vow, and my thoughts and feelings flowing within the inconceivable Dharma-ocean.
>
> (*Teachings*, IV. p. 616)

This is the background. The meaning of some of the vocabulary used so far may be unclear, but I shall explain them in due course. Now let us begin to answer some of the questions most often asked.

Ocean

PART ONE

Foundation

Ocean

Chapter One

The Heart of Buddhism: Trunk of the Tree

Please tell me something about Jodo-Shinshu Buddhism.

Jodo-Shinshu is one of the many schools of Buddhism, just as Lutheranism is one of the schools within Christianity. So, I shall first explain the basic teachings of Buddhism, and then of Jodo-Shinshu (from Chapter 4).

How would you, then, describe Buddhism?

Buddhism is a religion of *awareness*.

What do you become aware of?

We become aware of the principles of existence. These principles are the Dharma or teachings, the truths by which we try to think and live.

What are these principles?

There are many principles in Buddhism, for example the Four Noble Truths, the Dependent Co-arising, and the Four Marks of Existence. Among them, I select the Four Marks of Existence for beginners in Buddhism. Buddhist teachings can seem complicated, but I have an easy way to remember the Four Marks of Existence:

1) Life is a **B**umpy road,
2) Life is **I**mpermanent,
3) Life is **I**nterdependent,
4) Life is Fundamentally **G**ood.[2]

So, to remember the four, "Think BIIG!"

What is meant by "Life is a Bumpy road"?

We all experience disappointments, fear and sadness. Some of us hit more bumps than others, and we can't avoid them. These bumps are a natural part of our human existence. Sometimes we forget this or do not want to accept it, and we expect our road to be smooth. Buddhism describes these bumps (*duhkha*) as: 1) birth, 2) aging, 3) illness, 4) death, 5) being separated from loved ones, 6) having to associate with those we dislike, 7) not

---

2   Traditonally the four are expressed: 1) *anitya/anicca* (impermanence), 2) *duhkha/dukkha* (suffering; bumpy road), 3) *anatman/anatta* (egolessness; non-self), and 4) *nirvana/nibbana* (enlightenment). Here, I have reversed the order of the first two. Further, *anatman* is rendered "interdependence" rather than the more literal "egolessness," since "interdependence" makes more sense for our readers while still retaining its religious intent of urging seekers to become aware and to let go of their attachments.

getting what we desire, and 8) being attached to the five components (*skandha*)[3]; that we call "I" or "self." The five components are 1) physical elements and the senses, 2) feelings or sensations, 3) perception or conception, 4) mental formations or volition, and 5) consciousness.

We shouldn't turn away from these bumps. The bumps in our lives are not there to punish us for being evil or because we are failures. The bumps are there not to teach us lessons, though we can certainly use them in that way. If we face them we can learn from them and grow. These bumps are the stepping stones toward the ultimate Buddhist goal, which is to become Buddhas or be enlightened; in a more common language, to come to spiritual resolution.

What do you mean by "Life is Impermanent"?

Nothing stays the same from one moment to the next. This is true from the atoms that make up our physical world to the movements in the far off galaxies. Our social and political institutions are always changing as well. For example, who would have guessed, even a few years ago, that the mighty Soviet Union would crumble? Often the changes go unnoticed, but when we take stock, the many changes in our society have been enormous. Allow me to

---

3 The *skandhas* in Sanskrit (also translated "aggregates" or "heaps") refer to the five experiential and ever-changing components that make up "one's" reality at any given time. Suffering results when we falsely grasp at the components as the "self." For explanation, see *What the Buddha Taught,* pp. 20–23.

share an excerpt from a piece "For All Those Born Before 1945." What it shares is amusing but true!

We are survivors! Consider the changes we have witnessed! We were born before television, before penicillin, before polio shots, frozen foods, xerox, plastic contact lenses, Frisbees and the PILL. We were before radar, credit cards, laser beams, and ballpoint pens. Also, we were before pantyhose, dishwashers, clothes dryers, electric blankets, air conditioners, drip-dry clothes, and before man walked on the moon.

We got married before and then lived together. How quaint can you be? In our time, closets were for clothes, not for "Coming out of." ...We thought fast food was what you ate during Lent... For us, time-sharing meant togetherness...not computers and condominiums. A chip meant a piece of wood. Hardware meant hardware, and software wasn't even a word... Back then, "Made in Japan" meant "junk" and the term "Making Out" referred to how you did on your exam. In our day, grass was mowed, COKE was a cold drink and POT was something you cooked in... But WE SURVIVED! What better reason to celebrate![4]

---

4   June, 1995 issue of the Gardena Buddhist Church newsletter.

When we scan a past recalled by these provocative passages, we realize how significant and profound the changes have been. Impermanence is a fact of our societal life.

We experience impermanence most deeply on the personal level. We see changes in our relationships and in our bodies. This truth is apparent when we are forced to separate from our first love, or when we can no longer make that quick drive toward the basket on the basketball court. We really wake up when we see our first gray hair in the mirror and murmur to ourselves, "Wow, it's true! I, too, am subject to impermanence."

So are we to feel sad and helpless because everything is impermanent?

No, to the contrary, we become more fully alive by understanding the truth of impermanence! We shouldn't fight change with our desire to keep things the same. Our ego needs to allow life to flow forward. Every moment is the unfolding of life and different from the moment before. Every encounter in our life is special. Dr. Yutang Lin, a Buddhist teacher living in California, captures this Buddhist insight in a poem:

> *Suddenly I see that life could end*
> *at any moment!*
> *Once I realize that I am so close to death*
> *I am instantly free in life.*
> *Why bother to criticize or fight with others?*
> *Let me just be pure in mind and enjoy living!*[5]

---

5   Yutang Lin. *Two Practices of Impermanence (El Cerrito, California:*

The key line is "I am instantly free in life," which offers us a glimpse into the liberating benefits of becoming fully aware of the truth of impermanence. This awareness helps us to savor life even in the face of unwanted changes. For one thing, if things are going badly now, we can find hope in knowing that nothing stays the same and something new will enliven our hearts. A poem by Ms. Ok-koo Kang Grosjean, a friend and a Buddhist, captures this insight:

> *January 2nd.*
> *My heart lonely*
> *after my son leaves for school (college)*
> *I go out to the backyard.*
>
> *In the garden, deserted*
> *during last month's cold,*
> *red azaleas*
> *have bloomed.*
>
> *In that raging gale*
> *that blew off all the leaves*
> *how is it these tender flowers*
> *are safe?*
>
> *The heart,*
> *disquieted*
> *a little while ago,*
> *has eased*

Yutang Lin, 1992), p.8.

and in this quiet garden
peace of mind
blooms as azaleas.[6]

A mother's sadness on losing a son to college is soothed by the flower in her backyard. It's a good thing she had cultivated the awareness to be open to the next moment—the blooming azaleas!

How about the principle that "Life is Interdependent"?

We are a product of many influences that create who we are and how we feel. As waves are part of the ocean, we are part of the rest of the universe. Today, the principle of interdependence offers a rallying point for the environmental movement. Modern scientists are showing how the systems of nature are all linked together. Each system in nature needs all the others to stay alive. In human relations, the end of the cold war and the birth of a different world order are showing us that nations need one another to survive, too. We can see this in the economic area where even "made-in-America" cars have parts from many corners of the "global village."

Our failure to appreciate this truth fosters greater egotism and social isolation. We really do need others for our well-being. Our insistence on raw individuality at all times leads to neglect of our communities and loss of the

---

6   Ok-koo Kang Grosjean. *A Hummingbird's Dance* (Berkeley: Parallax Press, 1994), p. 5.

sense of belonging. Without connection to our communities, we find ourselves stripped of the values that give meaning to our lives.

I am using "interdependence" as a synonym for "non-self," which is a word that appears in many Buddhist books. The two words ("non-self" and "interdependence") point to the same truth. The Sanskrit (an ancient language of India) word for this principle is *anatman*. This is a difficult concept to accurately translate into English. That is why I translated "non-self" as "interdependence," which I feel is easier to understand and yet does not lose the original spiritual intent. *Anatman* is normally translated "non-self," "non-soul," "selfless," or "ego-less."[7]

Does that mean we sacrifice our individual selves?

Our individuality is retained without sacrificing or denying the self of the everyday world.[8] Buddhist can speak out confidently against violence, hatred, discrimination and excessive greed. Shakyamuni Buddha is well

---

7 This means that there is no unchanging, independent substance or entity (*atman*) associated with what we consider the "self." According to the Buddha, the "self" at any given moment is comprised of the five experiential and ever-changing components (See page 11). And no *atman* is to be found over and beyond the five components.

8 Robert Bellah and his coauthors speak of two kinds of individualism in their study of contemporary American ethos, utilitarian and aesthetic. The former refers to the self-centered mode, but here we take the latter meaning, which speaks to the sacredness of the individual. See their book, *Habits of the Heart*.

known for having opposed the caste system for its inherent abuses. So, the oppressed people of the world are not forced to accept their plight but are revitalized to speak out confidently to improve their conditions. Individuality shines within the interdependent network of existence like Indra's Net of Jewels. Each jewel becomes brighter, illuminated by other jewels. All the jewels are mutually made brighter. A net extends throughout the whole universe in all ten directions. At each "eye" of the net is a jewel. Each jewel is unique in its shape, color, and luster. At the same time, each jewel is related to all the other jewels on the net. Each jewel reflects the rays of all the other jewels of the net reciprocally.

How do we live less self-centered lives?

Well, that is what the Buddhist path is leading toward! If people are interested, they must walk the path with dedication. There is no magic wand, but I firmly believe that dedicated effort will enable us to live in ways that are far less self-centered.

Why? How does it help me if I lead a less self-centered life? Who else would take care of me if I do not?

I hear the same kind of question quite often. It's a good question. Buddhism is concerned primarily with the sufferings of an existential rather than a social or economic nature. The focus is on a vertical rather than a horizontal dimension. From this perspective, Buddhism encourages "a less self-centered life" in order to overcome the existential bumps (anxiety, suffering or pain) of aging, illness, death, not getting what we desire, etc. (see page 10). This less self-centered life reduces greed, hatred and ignorance, which in turn reduces our existential suffering. So, just as in the case of the Buddha, a less self-centered life helps us deal better with the existential questions of our lives.

However, this focus on existential suffering should not encourage us to ignore our socioeconomic needs, for we live at the intersection of the vertical and the horizontal. As laypersons, we must secure a livelihood for ourselves and for our families. We must take care of ourselves. This requires us to be quite self-centered and even be self-assertive at times. However, if our actions are influenced by Buddhist ideals, we will naturally become less self-centered even on this socio-economic level. We will, for example, devote more of our earnings to help others; or will engage in occupations that do not add to violence to others (manufacturing or handling of weapons of destruction).

What does the fourth principle, "Life is fundamentally Good" mean?[9]

With the right attitude or view, and despite the bumps, I can find much joy and meaning in my life. At times, though life seems bleak, I can make things brighter

---

9   This is not to deny injustices, cruelties and suffering that exist in our world. For this reason I have qualified this statement with "fundamentally." Buddhism is primarily concerned with how a person relates to the world and not to the objective world divorced from a person's subjective experience of it.

by remembering the Buddhist teachings. The Buddha tells us, "With our minds we make the world."[10]

He is saying that life is very much what you choose to make it. In a well known Buddhist metaphor, water appears differently according to the perceiver. To the hungry ghosts (those with meager awareness, beset by never-satisfied desires), the water is phlegm and pus; for a fish it is an abode and for a human something to drink. However, for a Bodhisattva who has realized deep awareness and compassion for others, the water is a bed of shimmering jewels! There is only one object, but there are four levels of awareness. The more we foster Bodhisattva awareness, the more we experience our lives as "fundamentally good"!

What about people who live in poverty? What about social/political injustice in our world? Are we supposed to think these sufferings are due to "wrong views" or "negative attitudes"?

---

10   This is part of a longer well-known passage from one of the earliest sutras (collection of sermons or discourses usually given by the Buddha), the *Dhammapada*:

With our minds, we make the world.
Speak or act with meanness, and unhappiness will follow you
as surely as a cart follows the ox that pulls it.

With our minds, we make the world.
Speak or act with kindness,
and happiness will follow you as surely
as a shadow follows the person who casts it.

These concerns you cite are certainly not to be ignored. They must be addressed. (see page 207) Their difficulties are not simply due to their unwholesome, or as you say, "wrong" spiritual views but are the product of numerous objective conditions. (See Chapt. 11 on Karma) However, from a Buddhist position these concerns cannot be effectively dealt with separate from our own spiritual cultivation.

How do the Four Marks of Existence work?

Our awareness of the Four Marks works like good shock absorbers on a car. How different is the ride of a car whose shocks are broken compared to a car with the best possible shocks? Good shocks help to soften the blow from the bumps. They keep our car from being damaged so we can keep moving along.

Experientially, they help us to flow with the events of life, and to lessen our natural urge to *control* life. We are then able to determine what can be changed and what we must let go into the flow of life. With unwholesome views, however, we cling rather than let go.

What are the unwholesome views?

People who expect life to be 1) smooth, 2) "mine" 3) always the same, and 4) lousy, have unwholesome views. They are going against the Four Marks of Existence. To help us remember this, I say "Think BIIG!" but "Don't Think SMAL!" (smooth, mine, always and lousy).

What is the connection between the Four Marks and the well-known Buddhist teaching of Four Noble Truths?

The Four Marks of Existence are included within the Four Noble Truths. The Four Noble Truths are:

1) We all experience suffering;
2) Suffering is caused by the Three Poisons of greed, hatred and delusion;
3) The end of suffering is nirvana;
4) The path to nirvana or enlightenment is the Eightfold Path.

Where in the Four Noble Truths are the Four Marks included?

Remember that the Fourth Noble Truth refers to the Eightfold Path. The Eightfold Path is made up of:

1) Wholesome view
2) Wholesome thought
3) Wholesome speech
4) Wholesome conduct
5) Wholesome livelihood
6) Wholesome effort
7) Wholesome mindfulness
8) Wholesome meditation.

The Four Marks of Existence are in the first truth, "wholesome view." To have "wholesome view" means to have the correct view of the world or the correct attitude toward life. You have the wholesome view if you are thinking BIIG. In review, the main principles are the Four Marks of Existence, the Four Noble Truths and the Eightfold Path.

Four Noble Truths

1 Suffering
2. Cause (reason)
3. Nirvana
4. Path ←――――――→ <u>Eight-Fold Path</u>

<u>**Four Marks of Existence**</u>

1. Wholesome View ←――――――→
2. Wholesome Thought
3. Wholesome Speech
4. Wholesome Conduct
5. Wholesome Livelihood
6. Wholesome Effort
7. Wholesome Mindfulness
8. Wholesome Meditation

1. Bumpy Road
2. Impermanence
3. Interdependence
4. Fundamentally Good

Isn't Buddhism pessimistic because the First Truth is "suffering"?

No. Please note that "suffering" is the starting point, but the goal is the state of nirvana. When we realize nirvana, our suffering ends and true joy emerges within. The main focus of Buddhist teachings and practices is the elimination of all suffering. The Buddha taught precisely in order to help others overcome suffering.

His teaching of Dependent Co-arising explains how suffering arises as well as how we can eliminate suffering. The twelve preconditions are 1) ignorance, 2) dispositions or karma-formation, 3) consciousness, 4) name-and-form or conditioned mental and physical phenomena, 5) the six sense faculties, 6) contact, 7) feeling or sensation, 8) desire, 9) clinging, 10) process of becoming, 11) rebirth, and the 12) sufferings of aging, dying, lamentation, pain, etc. Ignorance is the source of suffering. On the other hand, if ignorance is eliminated, suffering will cease to arise.

How can this explanation apply to my life today?

Let us take the example of seeing the first gray hair in the mirror, a sign that I, too, am growing old! It is a concrete example of my aging, the twelfth precondition and also one of the eight kinds of suffering (or bumps) specifically mentioned by the Buddha (See page 10). For some people, a gray hair is not a problem, but for me it was. This unpleasant feeling has its roots in ignorance, the first precondition. I lacked full wisdom about the truth of impermanence (see page 12). Surely, I have heard and read about this truth numerous times, but I knew it only with my head and not with my total being. Plus, I may wishfully on an unconscious level have thought, "No, it can't happen to me."

Based on this deep-seated ignorance, my gray hair triggered a chain of rapid psychological reactions (preconditions #2–6). I then experienced a clear unpleasant feeling (#7), followed by a desire for no gray hair (#8) (or hatred of gray hair, for desire and hatred are two sides of the same sheet). I further clung (#9) to the idea of not having a gray hair, that is, to continue to stay young. This clinging to a wishful, fixed image clashed with my reality, causing me to experience suffering, lamentation and pain (#10–12). The same process would apply to other examples of suffering, such as separation from our loved ones or meeting up with people we do not like.

However, through cultivation of the Buddhist path, ignorance can be replaced with wisdom. By eliminating ignorance, the rest of the chain reaction would not occur, and we do not experience suffering. Wisdom makes us realize that gray hair is a natural process of physical change, nothing less and nothing more. It is I who create suffering that really does not exist in reality. It is my delusion as well as my illusion!

The Buddha's disciples found this teaching extremely liberating and optimistic. They gained a fresh way of understanding the source of their suffering. Suffering was not brought about by gods, chance or fate. They were now in control of their destiny, for they found a path for overcoming suffering through their effort.

So, suffering in Buddhism does not refer so much to the suffering that is brought on by others. It appears much more psychological.

Yes, I believe that is a fair description. When I speak to non-Buddhist groups, someone in the audience often reminds me that we do not create our suffering. The sufferings of the poor and the victims of violence are not their creation! So, they understand suffering in mostly socioeconomic terms. I, therefore, explain that because suffering in Buddhism is existential in nature (e.g., aging, death, and relationships), the solution takes on a much more psychological rather than a sociological tone.

Going back to our first topic of awareness as the aim of Buddhism, what happens when we become more aware?

We become truly human when we are fully aware! This means we feel a deeper appreciation for that which sustains our lives. We see the need to make life better for all the living, not just humans. Because we know we are imperfect, we try to be mindful of how we act. We are aware that our actions have consequences.

When our awareness deepens so much that we go through a complete change for the good, it is called an "awakening," "enlightenment" or "nirvana." "Buddha" means "one who has become awakened." The goal of all Buddhists is to become a Buddha.

Does that mean humans can become a Buddha?

Yes. Shakyamuni Buddha, the founder of Buddhism, was born as a prince of a kingdom in the Himalayan foothills of Northeastern India around 560 B.C.E. (or B.C.) He realized enlightenment, became a Buddha, at the age of thirty-five. After that, he ministered and taught through Northeastern India for the next forty-five years. He remained actively engaged until his death around 480 B.C.E. So he actually lived on earth. He is neither a deity nor God.

Is he the fat, laughing Buddha? And do I get my wish by rubbing his tummy?

No, not quite. That laughing Buddha statue was created in China at least a thousand years after Buddha's death for the common people. It was modeled after a non-Buddhist god of prosperity. In India, Buddha was not shown in statue form until four hundred years after his death. Then, these statues showed the Buddha as a man of serenity, discipline, understanding and wisdom. They were not idols to be worshipped but examples of what Buddhists aspired to be and still aspire to be. In contrast, the laughing Buddha served to make the Buddha more human, accessible and relatable to the general public that included non-Buddhists.

So, Buddha and God are different?

Yes. Buddha is human, while God in the Western religious traditions is not human.

Do Buddhists believe in God?

Before I can answer that question, I must ask, what is meant by "God"? People have many ideas about who or what God is. Until I understand this, it is hard for me to answer. If God is defined primarily as cosmic compassion and wisdom, then some Buddhists (particularly Mahayana Buddhists—see page 47) may be inclined to say they believe in "God." But that will be a personal decision of a modern Buddhist. As for me, I would exercise a great deal of caution, making sure that "God" is clearly defined and acceptable to me as a Buddhist. On the other hand, if God is a supreme personal being who created the universe, lives in heaven, watches over me, and knows my thoughts and actions, then Buddhists clearly do not believe in God.

Then, Buddhists do not believe in anything supernatural?

No, that is not exactly what I meant to say. Instead of a personal divine creator, Buddhists have always spoken of an enlightened reality called "Dharma."

This Dharma as "reality" is the source for the Dharma as the "teaching" we talked about before (see page 9). The English translation of this Dharma (*dharmakaya, dharmata, dharmadhatu,* etc.) includes Law, Logos, Suchness, Truth, and Reality. In modern everyday language, this Dharma can be described as Life, Universe, Cosmic Compassion, Life-giving Force, or Energy. I like the word "Oneness" because it reminds us that the enlightened reality (Dharma) is not separate from us. We are actually one with Dharma. It's right under our feet, but we don't know it.

Please say a little more about this Oneness.

Just imagine that each of us is a jewel on Indra's net as talked about earlier (see page 17). We are part of the Oneness, which is not just an idea in our heads. We can all experience dimensions of Oneness in the many examples of caring we receive from our family and friends in our daily lives. Oneness is not separate from our experiences. Oneness is seen, touched, smelled, heard and tasted. Oneness expresses itself most directly and fully as the liberating spiritual light and energy to the most fervent and sensitive of spiritual seekers. For others, Oneness (as Compassion or Amida) can be experienced as the caring love of their family members or their friends, or as the beauty and wonder of nature (see pages 140, 159).

Does this mean that we are all Buddha, since we are all a part of the Indra's Net?

We are not all Buddhas right now, but we are all potential Buddhas. The Mahayana Buddhists expressed this in the teaching, "all sentient beings possess Buddha nature." Simply being part of Indra's Net of Jewels does

not make us Buddhas; we must, instead, fully awaken to
the spiritual caring and understanding that derive from
others on the net.

What is the relationship between Oneness and awareness?

The more we become aware, the more we realize
Oneness. This relationship is like that of the drowning
swimmer who discovered (awareness) the caring Ocean
(Oneness) when he let go of his striving. In actual Buddhist
life, we engage in some kind of practice to help us
realize this awareness.

How do Buddhists practice?

According to the Dharma, practice fosters wisdom
which in turn eliminates and replaces ignorance, the
cause of our suffering. Wisdom helps us to live life as it
really is, not how we wish it were. Buddhist tradition
talks about 84,000 ways to practice. All practices cultivate:
1) precepts, 2) meditation, and/or 3) wisdom.

The precepts are the rules of conduct, speech, and
thought. They give us a framework to focus our lives so
we can live the teaching. Practicing meditation helps us
to clear our minds and allows us to see the obstructions
of unwholesome views. Cultivating wisdom replaces unwholesome
views with insight, which frees us from
worry, pain, and negative thinking.

**Does Buddhism have a holy book like the *Bible* or
the *Koran*?**

There is no one book in Buddhism that serves the
same function as the *Bible* in Christianity or *Qur'an*

(*Koran*) in Islam. There is, however, a large encyclopedic set of scriptures called the *Tripitaka* (Three Baskets). The *Tripitaka* is a collection of *Sutras* (talks or sermons usually given by Shakyamuni Buddha), *Vinaya* (rules of behavior initially established by the Buddha), and *Abhidharma* (scholastic writings by disciples of later generations). The collection is about ten times the length of the *Bible*. Each school of Buddhism today uses a different section as its important scripture.

Then what commonalities are there among the different Buddhist schools?

All the different schools agree on the Three Treasures or Jewels (in Sanskrit, one of the ancient languages these texts were written in, it is called *Tri-ratna*). The Three Treasures are the Buddha, the Dharma (teachings), and the Sangha (Community of monks and nuns).[11]

---

11   Today, particularly in the West, "Sangha" has come to include the lay Buddhists.

Ocean

Chapter Two

Buddhism Today: A Personal View

What points about Buddhism do you like?

I find Buddhism appealing because it is voluntary, open, personal and peaceful.

By "voluntary" I mean it's not a "sin" to turn away from the Dharma or teaching. We make efforts to share the teachings and our experiences, but if people are not interested we simply wait for them to become interested. When the time is right they will seek answers to their questions. The Buddha called out, *"ehi passiko"* (come here and see!) if people are interested.

"Open" means that Buddhism is open-minded about other religions and sects. Buddhists think there are 84,000 ways to enlightenment. Of course, although Buddhists would like others to take an interest in the Dharma, they just don't think it's right to *force* people to take interest. What's more, we don't think people are doomed to be punished if they walk other paths.

By "personal" I mean that there is much value given to personal understanding. Dharma cannot come alive without speaking directly to our unique experience. We do not accept the Dharma blindly. We test how it works in our everyday life. Just before he died, the Buddha said, "Make *yourself* the light, and make the Dharma the light." Also he cautioned:

> Do not accept a statement on the ground that it is found in our books, nor on the supposition that "this is acceptable," nor because it is the saying of your teacher.[12]

But he did not mean to imply that we can do whatever we please because there is no standard. No, the standard is the Dharma. The Buddha was telling us to see how the teachings work in our lives before we accept them.

I am also impressed by how peaceful Buddhism is. Throughout history, Buddhists have taught not to be violent towards others just because they believed differently. In modern times the Dalai Lama of Tibet is a great example of a Buddhist leader acting peacefully. Even though the Chinese regime has taken over his Buddhist country and made life miserable for his people, the Dalai Lama works without rest to find a peaceful way to free his homeland.

---

12   *Anguttara-Nikaya* IV, 382.

This is not to claim that the Buddhist communities were or are *completely* immune from violent actions against each other. There have been skirmishes to be sure, but they were motivated more by institutional jealousies than doctrinal differences. I suppose all religious institutions sometimes fail to live up to the pure ideals of their teachings; Buddhism is no exception. It seems to me, however, that Buddhism has exhibited, relatively speaking, a high degree of peace that many observers, including non-Buddhists, regard as the hallmark of the tradition.

Are there any other points that you like?

Yes. I am attracted to the teaching that "All sentient beings possess Buddha nature."[13] This means that not only humans, but animals, birds, fish, and other creatures are all sacred and should be treated with respect. Humans do not have any right to rule over them. When their lives are taken so we can have food, we must be grateful to them for their sacrifice. The East Asian Buddhists expanded this way of thinking to even include inanimate things such as the mountains, rivers, grass, and soil.[14] We humans must also live well together. We are part of nature, not rulers of nature. We must cherish and protect it.

---

13   This view is expressed in the Mahayana texts that espouse the Buddha-womb or Buddha-nature thought, for example, *Mahaparinirvana-sutra*.

14   For example, see Shinran, *Notes on 'Essentials of Faith Alone.* (Kyoto: Hongwanji Int. Center, 1979), p. 42. "Thus, plants, trees, and land all attain Buddhahood."

What accounts for these qualities in Buddhism?

According to Prof. Gananath Obeyeskere, these qualities derive from the very nature of the religions that originated in India, particularly those of the lower Ganges valley in India such as Jainism and Buddhism. In regard to their central message, ethics and relationship to other religions, these Gangetic religions stand in contrast to western religions such as Christianity, Islam, Judaism, and Zoroastrianism. The contrast can be summarized as follows:

1. In the Western religions the prophet is the vehicle for communicating to the world the message of a transcendental God. In the Gangetic religions the ascetic formulates his own message, derived from his own inner experience of awakening. Gods and deities wield no great power and at best help to validate the message of the ascetic.

2. The ethics or morality is expressed as "commandment" in the former and as "precepts" in the Gangetic religions. The commandment is an expression of the God's will, while the precepts are followed because of their inherent rightness.

3. The above differences become more pronounced when they are institutionalized. Because the prophetic message comes from God, it takes on an uncompromising attitude toward the world and tends to see other messages as inferior. In contrast, because the ascetic message comes from inner realization of individual ascetics, it is vulnerable to com-

promise and revision and tends to regard others with tolerance.

4. The uncompromising character of the prophetic religions leads to conflict with the other religious and secular orders and threatens their leaders. On the other hand, the flexible character of Gangetic religions does not threaten the existing social order, for it is neutral and open towards it.[15]

There are, of course, limitations and exceptions to these generalizations, but I believe these points offer some explanations for the Buddhist features that we find today.

Yes, the explanation helps to clarify the historical roots in the differences between Buddhism and the Western religions. One major difference I see has to do with the teaching of reincarnation. Do Buddhists believe in reincarnation?

Some do and some don't. Some take it as fact, while others see it as symbolic. The idea of reincarnation goes back to ancient India. Buddhists in the past believed in this idea because it fit in with their worldview. Many people in the West have also believed in reincarnation, starting with the ancient Greek philosophers.[16] But in

---

15   Gananath Obeyeskere, *The Rebirth Eschatology and Its Transformation: A Contribution to the Sociology of Early Buddhism*, in Wendy Doniger O'Flaherty, *Karma and Rebirth in Classical Indian Traditions* (Berkeley: Univ. of Calif. Press), pp. 162–164.

16   "... the concept of rebirth occupied a central concern in Greek thought from the time of Phecerides of Ciro (6th cent. B.C.E.), the mentor of Pythagoros (c. 582–507 B.C.E.), and came into full flowering in the writings of Plato (427–347 B.C.E.) and

Buddhism belief in reincarnation (we prefer "transmigration" or "cycle of births and deaths") was not an absolute requirement for reaching the religious goal of enlightenment.

I think the idea of transmigration is used to explain some basic things about our existence; that is, each person's life is far more than just the years we spend in our present life. Each of us arrives here because of thousands of little things that have happened since the beginning of time. All those little things come together at just this moment so that we can be here right now. For us to even be here is a wonder that no logic can ever explain.

Another Buddhist teaching that we hear often is karma. What is karma?

Karma does not mean "fate" as is so often believed. Karma means "our action." There are numerous ways to explain karma, but basically it means that our mental and spiritual well-being is determined by our own actions (karma), not by fate, not by chance, not by miracle, and not by divine being. One is able to determine his or her spiritual well-being through his or her own actions; through what he or she thinks, says, and does. Karma is optimistic! (See Chapter 11 devoted to karma.)

By cultivating correct awareness about life, we gain an upper hand over the "ups and downs of life" and remain generally at peace with ourselves. Karma works some-

---

Plotinus (205–270 C.E.)." *Encyclopedia of Religion*, Vol. 12 (N.Y.: MacMillan Publishing Co.), 268A.

what like a computer data base. By inputting and storing more correct information, the data base expands our capability to resolve new problems that may arise. For example, by inputting "impermanence," we are able to cope far better than without it to the changes in our lives (e.g., illness, divorce). We then grow from those experiences through a conviction that "karma offers immense possibilities to create our lives!"

Do you pray?

Yes we do, but not to the same extent or in the same manner as in Western traditions. This is partly because we emphasize meditation and reflection more than prayer. The other reason, of course, lies in the absence of a supreme divine being to whom one can pray.

I understand there are many kinds of prayer in Christianity, including thanksgiving, blessing, intercession and invocation. In the Buddhist tradition, too, gratitude (similar to Christian "thanksgiving") plays a vital role in the thoughts and actions of Buddhists. This is especially true among the Jodo-Shinshu Buddhists for whom gratitude constitutes the primary motivation for much of their religious and worldly actions. Similarly, Buddhists seek blessings for the happiness of all beings. "May all beings be happy" is the constant refrain in the *Loving Kindness Sutta* (or *Sutra*) that is most frequently chanted as a blessing by Buddhists of Southeast Asian background. Also, the Buddhists do "intercede" on behalf of others when they hear about misfortunes of others, such as an illness. Particularly the Buddhists of Southeast Asian background mindfully direct their thoughts to others, "May they get well; may they be happy."

But our concern for them should not simply stop here. To pray is easy, but a true test of our concern for others lies in our deeds, such as visiting them at the hospital or assisting the family with the chores during trying times.

Do you celebrate Christmas?

Most American Buddhists celebrate Christmas as a national holiday that promotes charity and goodwill. While we do not put up nativities (display of the birth of Jesus), most put up Christmas trees and exchange gifts, especially when children are involved. As explained earlier, the openness of Buddhism encourages us to look beyond form to see the spirit behind rituals. The spirit of sharing, giving, and appreciation is deeply cherished in Buddhism.

What are the major Buddhists holidays?

The ones that are common to all the Buddhists have to do with the events of Shakyamuni Buddha's life: his birth, enlightenment and death. But Buddhist schools observe them on different dates. For example, the Theravada Buddhists from Southeast Asia observe all three events during what they call *Vesak* on the full moon of the fifth lunar month. Other Buddhists observe each of the three events on different dates; for example, Japanese schools observe Buddha's death on February 15th (Nirvana Day), his birth on April 8th (Hanamatsuri or Flower Festival) and his enlightenment on December 8th (Bodhi Day). Another major holiday for East Asian

Buddhists is *Ullambana* (*Yu-lan-p'en* or *Obon*) celebrated in July or August for expressing gratitude to their deceased family members.

Thank you. I feel I have a much better outline of the basic Buddhist teachings. It is often difficult to get a straight picture of Buddhism because I feel there are in the West some old images about your religion.

One good example of that are the views expressed by Pope John Paul II in his *Crossing the Threshold of Hope*.[17] I found the Pope's comments disappointing, particularly given his position in the world that cries out for greater understanding among groups. The Pope's views, in my opinion, reflect a stereotypical and superficial understanding of Buddhism held by many Westerners, particularly those of the older generation to which the present Pope belongs.

Could you give me an example from his book?

The Pope states, "The fullness of such a detachment is not union with God, but what is called nirvana, a state of perfect indifference with regard to the world" (p. 86). Nirvana, however, does not mean a total indifference to the world. "Indifference" implies "lack of interest" and "uncaring." To the contrary, Shakyamuni Buddha devoted forty-five long years to sharing the Dharma in order that others may realize the same joy and inner peace of nirvana. One of the very reasons for the success of the

---

17   John Paul II. *Crossing the Threshold of Hope*. (New York: Alfred A. Knopf, 1994), pp. 84–90.

early Buddhist community can be found in its desire and ability to forge strong ties with the lay community.

In Mahayana Buddhism (See Chapt. 3), the Bodhi-sattvas sacrificed their own complete enlightenment (nirvana) in order to be among others to lead them to liberation. Further, the living Buddhist exemplars that I know are far from being uninterested, but are passionately devoted to helping others. Of course, these enlightened ones are not enamored by materialism, politics and such worldly affairs, but that would be true also of the Christian saints as expressed in Jesus' statement: "*in* the world but not *of* the world."

Doesn't the Pope's remarks reflect the perception that Buddhism like other Asian religions is world-negating?

Yes. The Pope expresses this when he stated, "The 'enlightenment' experienced by Buddha comes down to the conviction that the world is bad, that it is the source of evil and suffering for man" (p. 85). The source of suffering is not the world. Rather it is our personal attachment rooted in greed, hatred and ignorance. The world is neither all positive nor negative, but how the world is experienced is dependent on one's outlook. "With my mind, I make the world" goes the famous *Dhammapada* passage. Buddhism is subjective or psychological in nature, for it is based on the optimism that we are capable of transforming the way we experience the world. The Pope imposes a more objective or metaphysical Christian framework in looking at Buddhism.

This perception that "the world is bad," I believe, is partly influenced by the failure to understand the meaning of "suffering." The Buddhist suffering (*duhkha*) is a state to be *overcome*, while Christians tend to understand suffering as *a way of life* of a true Christian. "Suffering" is a virtue. In the Sermon on the Mount, we hear Jesus state, "Blessed are those who are humble, those who are just, those who try to do right, those who *suffer*—all of them will be rewarded in the Kingdom of Heaven" (emphasis added). It is, then, no great surprise that Christians often see Buddhism as a religion of pessimism, since "suffering" appears as the first truth in its hallmark doctrine, the Four Noble Truths. But that is a mistaken view.

Did you find problematic any other views expressed by the Pope?

Yes. The Pope believes that Buddhism is not as involved as Christianity (along with science) in the active attempt to transform the world. God and Christ are the driving force for change: "The truth about God the Creator of the world and about Christ the Redeemer is a powerful force which inspires a positive attitude toward creation and provides a constant impetus to strive for its transformation and perfection" (p.88). While I am in agreement with this observation that Western civilization exhibited an active push toward "transformation and perfection," it is curious that the Pope gives Christianity credit along with the Greek philosophical traditions as being the roots of science and technology. I would, of course, not deny any Christian contribution to the social transformation of the Western world, but even a cursory study of European history reveals a long and intense confrontation between the Church and the Renaissance/enlightenment movement that directly lead to the development of modern science.[18]

Do you feel that these perceptions about Buddhism will soon go away?

That the Pope has not gone beyond the mistakes of earlier Western bias toward Buddhism is disappointing and unfortunate. The Pope's views follow those of Max Weber, a noted sociologist of religion who helped in shaping the perception that Buddhism is concerned only with personal salvation but not with the welfare of others in society. This is certainly misguided (See pages 207). But I have reasons for hope. In recent years, for example, the progress in the studies of comparative religion and Buddhist Christian dialogue[19] has contributed to a more sympathetic and accurate understanding of Buddhism in the West. This has no doubt been helped by the enormous increase in the number of books and magazines on Buddhism for the general, nonacademic readership.[20]

---

18   As a poignant example of this tension between the two camps, the Catholic Church finally pardoned Galileo in 1995 for his "incorrect" ways.

19   For example, an academic association called the Society for Buddhist Christian Studies boasts a membership of approximately 400 members, publishes an annual journal, meets annually in conjunction with the American Academy of Religion and convenes a major conference of its own approximately every three years.

---

20 For example, *Tricyle: The Buddhist Review* (quarterly) presently
claims a circulation of approximately 40,000 readers and growing.

Ocean

Chapter Three

Buddhist Development: Branches of the Tree

Your answers so far haven't been distinctively Jodo-Shinshu, have they?

You're right. Jodo-Shinshu as part of the greater Buddhist tradition shares the basic assumptions and insights of other Buddhist schools. The questions so far have dealt with the trunk of the Buddhist tree. I like to think of Jodo-Shinshu as being a flower on that tree.

Where does the Jodo-Shinshu school fit within the overall development of Buddhism?

Today there are two major branches of Buddhism. One is called Theravada (School of Elders), which is dominant in Sri Lanka, Burma, Thailand, Cambodia, and Laos. The other is called the Mahayana (the Larger Vehicle), which is practiced in China, Japan, Korea, Mongolia, Taiwan, Tibet, and Vietnam.[21] Both branches trace their roots to the original teachings of Shakyamuni Buddha. Buddha himself belonged to no specific school, just as Jesus was not a Roman Catholic, an Eastern Orthodox or a Protestant.

Mahayana Buddhism in China gave birth to many schools during the sixth century including the Pure Land. The Pure Land school along with Ch'an (Zen) became two of the most popular and enduring traditions in China.

The Pure Land teaching crossed over to the Japanese islands as early as the eighth century.[22] Some four hundred years later, the Jodo-Shinshu school, a form of Pure Land Buddhism based on the teachings of Shinran Shonin (1173–1263), was born. "Jodo-Shinshu" means "the true essence of Pure Land [Buddhism]." The school is also known by its shortened names, "Shinshu" or "Shin."

What is the main characteristic of the Theravada branch?

I would say the important role of the monks[23] is the main characteristic of Theravada. Perhaps, you have seen

---

21 Some people speak of Vajrayana (Thunderbolt Vehicle) as the third branch, but I agree with some scholars who see Vajrayana as part of Mahayana.

22 I am here including the scholastic commentaries on Pure Land writings by the Buddhists of the Nara period, which were soon followed in the ninth century by the transmission of Pure Land practices within the Tendai school.

23 There no longer exists a legitimate order of nuns in the Theravada countries since their line of transmission was broken in 1017 C.E. when India invaded Sri Lanka and persecuted

scenes of the saffron-robed monks meditating in the mon-asteries or on their morning round of collecting alms in the streets. These monks are considered to have the best position to realize enlightenment in this life. The layper-sons play the role of supporters, in the hope that in some future lives they will become monks themselves.

Many years ago, I too led the life of a novice monk for three months in a monastery in Bangkok, Thailand. I still have many fond memories, particularly the stillness of the predawn morning, the aroma of the food being placed in my alms bowl, the genuine devotion of the laywomen, and the coolness of the ground as my bare feet paced mindfully through the town streets. I have nothing but respect for the monks who dedicate their lives to over-come greed, hatred, and ignorance. I marvel at their self-reliance, for they exemplify the Buddha's final words, "Make yourself an island (or light) and make the Dharma your light." I could not be as self-reliant; I needed people too much.

How is the Mahayana branch different from the Theravada branch?

Mahayana Buddhists place more emphasis than the Theravada Buddhists on the idea that laypersons (not only monks and nuns[24]) can realize enlightenment. The Ma-

---

Buddhism. Attempts to restore the order in modern times have not met with success. In actual practice, the white-robed female practitioners in Thailand, for example, play vital roles in the life of Buddhist communities.

24 Attempts to "revive" the line of nuns (*bhikhuni*) have not been

hayana Buddhists then look to an enlightened group called the "Bodhisattvas" to lead as many people to enlightenment as possible. These Bodhisattvas voluntarily put off becoming Buddhas themselves in order to assist all beings to attain enlightenment.

When did Mahayana Buddhism start?

Most scholars believe it started sometime in the first century B.C.E. (or B.C.), about 400 years after the death of the Buddha. The Mahayana Buddhists believe that their teachings express the true intent of what the Buddha taught. In their view, all beings have the potential to become Buddhas, and called this potentiality "Buddha nature." The Mahayanists offered a broad gate with hope for all beings. So they thought of themselves as the "Larger Vehicle" and criticized the older schools as "Hinayana" (Smaller Vehicle).[25]

A number of Mahayana branches developed within the next five hundred years in India, mostly centered around specific sutras or set of sutras. For example, the *Prajna-paramita* (Perfection of Wisdom) *Sutras* led to the Madhyamika (Middle [Path]) school founded by Nagarjuna (ca. 150–250 C.E.). Another set of sutras that

---

universally accepted by the Theravada hierarchies in Southeast Asia and in North America.

25 The Theravada Buddhists who are today in Southeast Asia were long gone from India when the Mahayanists came on the scene. Thus, the pejorative "Hinayana" referred to other earlier schools but not to the Theravadins.

included the *Sandhinirmocana Sutra* inspired a school called the Yogacara (Yoga Practice) or Vijnanavada (Teaching of Consciousness Only). Two brothers, Asanga and Vasubandhu (ca. 400 C.E.), were the key figures of this school. The *Lotus Sutra*, on the other hand, did not contribute to the formation of a doctrinally-based school in India, but its teaching of the One Vehicle and its literary beauty continue to have major influences in East Asia. The *Avatamsaka* (Garland) *Sutra* with its teaching of interdependence also did not lead to a school in India, but its impact outside India has been enormous.[26]

Please say a little more about Pure Land Buddhism.

The Pure Land tradition is part of the Mahayana branch, and started around the first century C.E., probably in Northwestern India. Its teaching is expressed in the *Larger Sukhavativyuha Sutra*, and strongly stresses the Mahayana ideal of enlightenment for everyone. The early Pure Land Buddhists felt that if everyone is to be enlightened, the teachings have to be for men and women strapped down to family life and who often live in a world full of wars, famine and political instability. Pure Land Buddhists still think so today.

The Pure Land Buddhists found hope. Through simpler practices, they could look forward in their next life to a birth in a special realm called *Sukhavati* (the Realm of

---

26 See Robinson, Richard and Willard Johnson. *The Buddhist Religion: A Historical Introduction* (Belmont, Ca.: Wadsworth Publishing Company, 1970), 65ff.

Serene Bliss) Pure Land. There, they are able to concentrate on completing their training in a perfect environment with the help of a Buddha called Amitabha (in Japanese "Amida") and Bodhisattvas. All those born in the Pure Land are assured of quickly becoming Buddhas. Many elect to return as Bodhisattvas in this and other worlds of birth-and-death (*samsara*) to help others realize the same spiritual liberation. Pure Land Buddhists believe their teaching shows the true intent of Shakyamuni Buddha: compassion, expressed as enlightenment for everyone. (See Chapter 10 on Pure Land)

How did Pure Land Buddhism develop afterwards?

It became a distinct school in China from about the fifth and sixth centuries and continues to this day as an important stream within the Buddhism of China. In fact, the number of Buddhists (lay and even monks and nuns) who engage in Pure Land practices is enormously large. They are also found in Tibet, Vietnam, Taiwan, Korea, and Japan in large numbers and probably make up the largest Buddhist segment in the world.

Pure Land teachings reached Japan as early as the eighth century, and developed gradually in the two centers of Buddhism: Nara and Mt. Hiei. Mt. Hiei, especially, produced many important scholar monks who practiced and taught Pure Land teachings. But it was Honen (1133–1212) who created a school that focused solely on the Pure Land teachings.(See Chapt. 5 on history.) Honen was the foremost leader of the new Pure Land movement that included not only peasants but also warriors and aristocrats. Shinran Shonin was one of Honen's devoted disciples. Shinran's disciples and descendants established the Jodo-Shinshu school, which has not only survived but is one of the largest Buddhist schools in Japan today.

Where does Zen fit in?

Zen is another sub-branch of Mahayana. It became a distinct school in China around the same time (seventh century) as the Pure Land school. In Japan, both schools emerged again, in the early Kamakura period (1185–1333). Today, both of these schools continue to be two of the most dominant streams in Japan as well as in East Asia. In China, Korea and Vietnam, monks and nuns generally engage in Zen meditative practice but also include some forms of Pure Land devotion in their daily regimen.

What are the major Japanese Buddhist schools that now have branches in North America?

There are only a handful of temples from the Shingon and Tendai schools. Honen's Jodo school is represented by a fairly good number of temples, particularly in Hawaii. The Rinzai branch of Zen has far fewer adherents than the Soto branch of Zen. The Jodo-Shinshu school is the largest and oldest, and claims the largest segment of the Japanese-descended community as its members. The older Nichiren school is sparsely represented, but its modern offshoots, Reiyukai, Rissho Koseikai and the Sokagakkai, have large followings.

Now that we have talked about the trunk, the major branch (Mahayana), and the minor branch (Pure Land), we are ready to talk about one of the flowers: Jodo-Shin-shu.

PART TWO

Legacy

Ocean

Chapter Four

Shinran Shonin: A Humble Challenger

Who is the founder of the Jodo-Shinshu school?

His name is Shinran Shonin (1173–1263). He lived during the Kamakura period (1185–1333), a time of momentous political and social changes in Japan. The Jodo-Shinshu developed out of the Jodo school which was founded by Honen, Shinran's teacher.

Tell me about Shinran Shonin. What does his name mean?

The name "Shinran" is made up of two Chinese characters meaning intimate or related (*shin*) and exquisite bird (*ran*). They come from the names of two eminent teachers in his spiritual lineage, one an Indian, Vasubandhu or Tenjin (or shin)[27] (5th century), and the

---

27   "jin" is also read "shin" which makes up "Shin" in "Shinran."

other a Chinese, T'an-luan or Don<u>ran</u> (476–542) in Japanese.

"Shonin" is an honorific title meaning honored person, eminent teacher or great master, an expression of respect by his followers. I'm sure he would have felt uncomfortable with such a title. He was a humble man who called himself "Gutoku," meaning the unshaven ignorant one.[28]

What qualities inspire you about Shinran Shonin?

I often speak of them as the "4 H's of Shinran": Honesty, Householder, Humility and Here-and-now.

By "honesty," I mean that he saw himself as he was and told the truth as he saw it. Despite twenty years of training as a monk, he was honest enough to tell the world that he was unfulfilled as a monk. He admitted that he was filled with ordinary selfish feelings:

> I know truly how grievous it is that I, Gutoku (the stubble-haired ignorant) Shinran, am sinking in an immense ocean of desires and attachments and am lost in vast mountains of fame and advantage.
>
> *(Teachings* II, 279)

---

28 "Gu" means ignorant, but obviously not in terms of knowledge. He used the terms within the context of spiritual realization, which I shall in later chapters refer to as "foolishness." "Toku" literally means "stubbled-haired," a term Shinran used in connection with his status as being "neither monk nor lay" upon being exiled and stripped of his monk status.

By "householder," I mean that Shinran Shonin's honesty about himself led him to marry and to have children, and yet pursue the Dharma as a householder. There were several founders of Buddhist schools who lived in Japan about the same time Shinran did, but Shinran is the only one who had a family. He is easy for me to relate to because he was a householder.

Shinran Shonin's "humility" comes across clearly when he says, "I do not have a single disciple," (*Tannisho*, p. 11) even though there were many followers who looked up to him as their teacher. He felt he could not take credit because their reason for seeking his guidance was not his own doing, but the workings of Amida Buddha. How refreshing he is compared to many self-serving religious teachers, both past and present!

By "here-and-now," I am referring to his focus on this life. The teachers before him emphasized the future life in the Pure Land. They neglected the spiritual change that is possible in the present life. They gave all their attention to death-bed rituals and visualizations, hoping to ensure birth in the Pure Land. For them, the Pure Land was a realm located billions of Buddha realms to the west. Those who were born in the Pure Land after death would find a place where it would be easy to do the practices needed to become a Buddha. Shinran Shonin took a radically different approach. He focused on the here-and-now and rejected the importance of the deathed rituals. Life would be nerve-wracking if the seekers had to wait to the end of their lives to know for sure about their spiritual fate. Instead, the assurance of complete enlightenment occurs with the spiritual transformation called Shinjin awareness. This awareness can come anytime in the life of the seeker. So, the seeker no longer worries about her spiritual destiny and is able to engage her daily life with greater confidence and optimism.

Do these traits make Shinran Shonin stand apart from other Buddhist figures?

Yes. In my view, these traits make him stand out, especially his householder and marital status. He is, nevertheless, still firmly rooted in the Buddhist tradition. Remember the four appealing qualities about Buddhism: voluntary, open, personal, and peaceful? Shinran Shonin showed them in his actions and words:

Voluntary: Some of his followers traveled hundreds of miles from the Tokyo area to Kyoto to ask if he knew of teachings other than the Jodo-Shinshu way. He replied emphatically, "No," since for a foolish person such as he, there was no other path. He did not, however, force them to accept his way. He wanted them to decide for themselves.

> Now, whether you accept the Nembutsu, entrusting yourself to it, or reject it, that is your own decision.
>
> (*Tannisho*, p. 7)

Open: Speaking to the same group of followers, Shinran Shonin encouraged them to meet with teachers of other schools if they were not satisfied with what he had to say:

If that be the case (you suspect that there is a better teaching), there are many eminent scholars in the monasteries of Nara and Mount Hiei, so you should go see them and ask them in detail about the way to attain birth in the Pure Land.

(*Tannisho*, p. 6)

Personal: This quality in Shinran finds expression in his famous utterance:

When I ponder the compassionate vow of Amida, established through five kalpas of profound thought, it was for *myself, Shinran, alone*.

(*Tannisho*, p. 35)

He is certainly not monopolizing the teaching for himself to the exclusion of others. Rather, based on his awareness about his own imperfect nature after a long hard search, he decided that the teaching was tailor-made for him. He was not in any position to speak for anyone else. The statement was a deeply personal admission, tested against his own experience.

The Buddhist appeal has always been primarily to the individual. A Buddhist is encouraged to try to clean up his own backyard before he points out or even tries to help clean up someone else's backyard.

Peaceful: Shinran expressed his peaceful nature through his sense of intimate connection with the animals, fish, and nature. At a time when most people were only thinking of their own family or clan, he saw all living creatures, both human and nonhuman, as members of his family:

> All beings have been fathers and mothers, brothers and sisters, in the timeless process of birth-and-death.
>
> *(Tannisho,* p. 10)

Shinran's view of the world encompassed the plants and even the physical world as brimming with spiritual life:

> Tathagata (Buddha) fills the hearts and minds of the ocean of all beings. Thus, plants, trees, and land all attain Buddhahood.
>
> *(Notes on "Essentials of Faith Alone,"* p. 42)

And as his life was coming to an end, he requested, "Throw my ashes in the Kamo River and feed me to the fish."

I read that Shinran Shonin's teaching is similar to Martin Luther's. Was it?

Many religious scholars agree that Shinran's teachings are like those of Martin Luther (1483–1546), the most famous Protestant reformer. Shinran and Luther do share similar understandings regarding 1) human nature, 2) ultimate truth and 3) the source of spiritual resolution. (See page 109)

I often teach classes of students studying for the ministry. The students are of many different faiths. Once, in my class on Jodo-Shinshu, a group of young Lutheran seminarians taking the course blurted out, "Your teaching is just like ours!" I praised them for seeing how Shinran and Luther are alike, but also pointed out some differences.

Then in jest, I said, "You know, it's actually Shinran Shonin who influenced Martin Luther, because Shinran lived about three hundred years earlier! Did you know Luther was a reincarnation of Shinran!" The class, made up of equal numbers of Buddhists and Christians, roared with laugher. They enjoyed sharing mutual respect for each other's traditions and were willing to accept that they were alike in some ways and different in others.

I understand that like Martin Luther, Shinran rebelled against the established religious order.

Yes, he was critical of the Buddhist clergy of his time as seen in this poem:

> *The monks and masters of today*
> *Are like low-grade servants,*
> *And the term "monks and masters" is*
> *synonymous with vulgarity.*[29]

In this poem Shinran must have been talking about the corruption and decadence on Mt. Hiei, where he spent twenty years from age nine to twenty-nine. Mt. Hiei was a major center of Buddhist learning and practice during his time. The bad behavior of the monks and teachers who lived there was one reason he decided to leave.

---

29   This poem is found in the *Shozomatsu-wasan,* translated by Norihiko Kikunaga. *Shinran: His Life and Thought* (Los Angeles: The Nembutsu Press, 1972), p. 62.

Did he try to reform Mt. Hiei in the way that Luther tried to reform the Catholic church?

Shinran Shonin did not challenge the establishment directly. When he left the monastery at the age of twenty-nine, he wielded no influence. Luther, on the other hand, was a renowned cleric and a professor at the University of Wittenburg.

Instead of challenging the establishment, Shinran directed his energies to answering his personal religious questions. His questions were finally answered when he became a disciple of Honen Shonin who taught a new kind of Pure Land Buddhism. Honen spoke of salvation for all beings regardless of spiritual and ethical ability. So, as a committed member of the new religious movement, Shinran worked to bring hope to all beings regardless of wealth, class, or education. In that process, he worked to effect changes in the Buddhist establishment.

At what other times may we see the challenger in him?

In 1207 the leadership of the new Pure Land movement led by Honen, was exiled from Kyoto (national capital and center of Buddhism). Shinran Shonin who was among them was sent to the Echigo area in Northern Japan. The exile was part of the growing persecution by the secular authorities, brought on by the jealousy and fears felt by the older established schools. Shinran Shonin expressed his outrage toward the high government officials and even toward the emperor. We who live in modern times cannot fully appreciate the courage that it took to attack the emperor! Shinran Shonin wrote:

The emperor and his ministers, acting against the dharma and violating human rectitude, became enraged and embittered. As a result, Master Genku (Honen)... and a number of his followers, without receiving any deliberation of their (alleged) crimes, were summarily sentenced to death or were dispossessed of their monkhood, given (secular) names, and consigned to distant banishment. I was among the latter.

(*Teachings* IV, pp. 613-614)

Again, Shinran and Luther share a common bond in that they both left the monastic path, married, and had many children. Please talk about the significance of Shinran's marriage.

Shinran Shonin is known as one of the first famous Buddhist monks to set aside his monk's robes and marry. While it is true there had been married priests called "shami," they were seldom officially approved as monks of established temples. All monks had to be approved and registered by the government. What makes Shinran Shonin's marriage important is that he was a former monk of the mighty Tendai school (one of the two dominant Buddhist schools of the period, along with Shingon) and went on to found a major school whose clergy, from its beginning, were married priests. Among those who founded the major schools of the Kamakura period, Shinran was unique in this regard. For example, Honen, who founded the Jodo school; Eisai, who founded the Rinzai Zen school; Dogen, who founded

63

the Soto Zen school; Nichiren, who founded the Nichiren school; and Ippen, who founded the Jishu, were all celibate monks.

Shinran married sometime during the four year exile after losing his monk status. His wife, Eshinni, was a well-educated woman, as seen by her writings. A collection of her letters was discovered in 1921.[30] Her letters give us important information that fills in some of the gaps in our knowledge about her husband.

Between them, they had six children: daughter (Woman of Oguro), son (Zenran;), daughter (Myoshin), son (Arifusa), daughter (Zenni) and daughter (Kakushinni).[31]

Why did he marry?

Because we have no direct statement by Shinran, we do not know the exact reasons with certainty. However, we do know that his teacher Honen did not prevent his students from marrying as he admonished:

> People should always live by creating the proper conditions for being able to say the Nembutsu. If you cannot say the Nembutsu as a celibate, say it by getting married. If you

30 See the book by Yoshiko Ohtani (refer to the bibliography section) for further information on her life and her letters. Prof. James Dobbins is currently completing his book on Eshinni.

31 Some scholars believe that Shinran was married (prior to Eshinni) to the daughter of the Regent Kujo Kanezane and had between them a daughter named Hanni.

cannot say it by being married, say it as a celibate.

... Food, clothing, and shelter are necessary only insofar as they create the proper condition for people to say the Nembutsu. (*Wago-toroku*)

What proved most important for members of the new Pure Land movement was the ability to devote themselves to the practice of Nembutsu. Honen did not specify a particular type of life-style for he allowed celibacy or married life, wanderer or sedentary life, and solitary or collective practice. Honen himself chose to be a monk.

Given this view toward marriage, any number of developments in his life could have led to his decision to marry. Scholars often cite the vision Shinran Shonin had just after he left the Tendai monastery at the age of 29 and just before joining Honen's movement. In the vision, Prince Shotoku (the 7th century patron saint of Japanese Buddhism) conveys to Shinran a message from Kannon (Avalokiteshvara), "You shall take a wife as the consequence of your past karmic life. I will be that wife. I shall guide you, so that you will lead an exemplary life and at death enter the Pure Land." Scholars also mention the impact that the exile (at the age of 35) might have had on Shinran, for he was stripped of his status as a monk. He would later write about his new status as "neither monk nor lay" (*hiso-hizoku*). This category of religious seekers was not unlike the Shamis mentioned earlier. These Shamis considered themselves as being neither monks nor laypersons and were often married with children. Shinran is reported to have admired one such recluse, Kyoshin of Kako.

What did Shinran Shonin do after he was pardoned?

Shinran, along with Honen and his other disciples, was pardoned by the government four years after he was banished. Perhaps the authorities felt that the exile had dealt an adequate blow to the rebellious, surging Pure Land movement. After his pardon he wanted very much to return to the capital to rejoin his teacher Honen. Before he could return, however, he learned that his esteemed teacher had died. Honen's death left him without any compelling reason to return to Kyoto. He then turned his energies to spreading Honen's teaching in the remote regions of Japan.

He decided to move even farther away from the capital to Kanto, the region that includes present-day Tokyo. With a large family, his move to the hinterlands must have entailed financial and physical sacrifices. Shinran spent the next nineteen years sharing the Dharma with others. He succeeded in nurturing a group of dedicated disciples.

He could easily have returned to the comforts and security of the capital, but instead he took the misfortune of the exile and transformed it into an opportunity. His risks and sacrifices gave him a rare opportunity to work with peasant followers who needed simple, direct and concrete answers. The harsh living conditions of the region must have required him to be even more down-to-earth. Speaking gratefully about his work, Shinran Shonin later said:

> If I had not been exiled, how would I have been able to teach the people of this remote area (the way of the Nembutsu)?[32]

Historians say that Shinran disowned his son. What does that say about him?

I find Shinran Shonin to be a man of high principles. He would not compromise the integrity of his religious beliefs. He expected the same high standard of his disciples, especially those who were teachers, and members of his family. When his son, Zenran, continued to mislead the followers by advocating wrong teachings[33] for his selfish gains, Shinran could see no other choice but to rebuke and disown him:

> To lie to me, Shinran, is none other than to kill your father, which is one of the Five Grave Offenses.[34]

---

32 Appears in Shinran's biography, *Den'ne*, written by Kakunyo (3rd Honganji abbot). English translation is from Kikumura's *Shinran: His Life and Thought*, p. 126.

33 While the exact nature of Zenran's teachings has not been fully determined, it is generally believed that he advocated the idea of "licensed evil" that advocated purposely committing evil acts since Amida's Vow embraced precisely those who are evil. Shinran condemned this view admonishing, "Do not take poison just because there is antidote."

34 Translated by the author from *Jodo-Shinshu Seiten*. (Kyoto: Hongwanji shuppan-bu, 1988), p. 755.

Shinran Shonin seems to have been a good family man, because both his wife and his youngest daughter speak of him with deep affection and respect. Therefore, he must have agonized over his decision to disown Zenran. Any parent who had to make such a decision would be deeply hurt. I am the father of three children, and I cannot imagine what it would be like to disown any one of them.

Which one quality about Shinran Shonin are you most attracted to?

If I must choose just one, I would say his honesty to admit to his weaknesses, failings and inadequacies. Today such admission of honesty is rare. We experience so much societal pressures to be exactly the opposite: strong and successful at all costs and seemingly confident. These "virtues" in turn propel us to seek happiness by going farther, moving faster and acquiring more.

In this sea of uneasiness, Shinran Shonin shows us how we need not succumb to these pressures. We can be honest by being truthful to ourselves with all our imperfections. We need not be someone else or get somewhere, for we are able to find resolution just as we are. From this peaceful center within, like that of a hurricane, Shinran Shonin moved dynamically outward to question and challenge the forces that undermined the Buddhist ideals.

Chapter Five

Historical Legacy: Ten Watershed Events from India to North America

Could you tell me a little more about how Jodo-Shinshu evolved to what it is today?

Let me answer that by citing ten watershed events that, in my personal view, have helped to shape the tradition as we know it today.

1. Circa 500 B.C.E.: Buddha Delivers a Sermon on Amida Buddha.[35]

According to the *Larger Pure Land Sutra*, Shakyamuni Buddha delivered a sermon on the sacred story of Bod-

---

35   This dating and its association with the historical Buddha would be difficult to substantiate (as with all other Mahayana sutras) from a strict historical point of view, but here we are following the Jodo-Shinshu traditional understanding.

hisattva Dharmakara (Dharma Storehouse), who eventually becomes Amitabha (in Japanese, Amida) Buddha. As a Bodhisattva he sets out to liberate his fellow sentient beings. He does this by sharing his immense storehouse of merit with those who earnestly desire to become enlightened.[36] Although sentient beings lack sufficient positive karma of their own, they are able to share in the Bodhisattva's stock of positive karma. They are then able to be born in the Pure Land to realize complete enlightenment. The *Larger Sutra* speaks of the events surrounding the sermon as follows:[37]

One day Shakyamuni Buddha dwelt on the Vulture Peak in the City of Rajagriha with thousands of his disciples. Venerable Ananda rose from his seat and knelt before the Buddha to address him:

> "World-Honored One, today all your senses are radiant with joy, your body is serene and glorious, and your august countenance is as

---

36 Mahayana Buddhism has stressed an earlier doctrine that the positive results of one's karma are transferable (*parinama*) to others. The idea of the Bodhisttvas directing their stock of positive karmic merit to liberate all sentient beings make up the motivation of their vows and their very existence. Thus, karma should not be seen as confined just to the individual. For an excellent modern discussion of "transcendental" spiritual forces, see Malcom David Eckel. *To See the Buddha: A Philosophical Quest for the Meaning of Emptiness* (Harper: San Francisco, 1992).

37 The descriptions and citation in this section are based on Hisao Inagaki, *The Three Pure Land Sutras: A Study and Translation* (Kyoto: Nagata bunshodo, 1994), pp. 227-255.

majestic as a clear mirror whose brightness radiates outward and inward....I have never seen you look so superb and majestic as to-day....For what reason does your countenance look so majestic and brilliant?"

Hereupon the Buddha said to Ananda:

"Tell me, Ananda, whether some god urged you to put this question to the Buddha or whether you asked about his glorious countenance from your own wise observation."

Ananda replied to the Buddha:

"No god came to prompt me. I asked you about this matter of my own accord."

The Buddha responded:

"Well said, Ananda. I am very pleased with your question. You have shown profound wisdom and subtle insight in asking me this sagacious question out of compassion for sentient beings....The reason for my appearance in the world is to reveal teachings of the Way and save multitudes of beings by endowing them with true benefits....Ananda, listen carefully. I shall now expound the Dharma."

Ananda replied, "Yes, I will. With joy in my heart, I wish to hear the Dharma. I shall listen with all my heart."

Then, the Buddha began to speak about a Buddha named World-Sovereign-King (Lokeshvara-raja) who

was the last in the line of fifty-three Buddhas, all of whom
lived in the incalculably remote past. When World-Sovereign-King Buddha delivered a talk, a king in the audience was so inspired by the talk that he decided to
renounce the throne and enter the life of a monk. He was
named Dharmakara (Storehouse of Dharma), and with
his superior abilities he excelled in his practices. One day,
Dharmakara requested World-Sovereign-King Buddha
to give him instructions so that he might establish a Pure
Land where beings from every corner of the universe
could be born. This Pure Land would enable them to
realize enlightenment in an environment most ideal for
spiritual cultivation.

Upon thorough instructions from his teacher, Monk
Dharmakara contemplated for a full five eons (*kalpas*)
and decided on a course of practice for the establishment
of an ideal Pure Land called *Sukhavati* (Realm of Bliss).
He then announced his plans through a set of forty-eight
vows, which described the physical attributes of the Pure
Land, the qualities and requirements of the beings to be
born there and the attributes of the Amida Buddha and
the Bodhisattvas who dwell there as spiritual teachers.
Amida Buddha was to be the name of Monk Dharmakara
when he fulfilled all the vows to become Buddha. The
eighteenth vow in particular is central to the Jodo-Shinshu teaching and thus is referred to as the Primal or
Original Vow. It declares:

> If, when I attain Buddhahood, sentient be-
> ings in the lands of the ten directions who
> sincerely and joyfully entrust themselves to me,
> desire to be born in my land, and contemplate[38]
> on my name even as many as ten times, should
> not be born there, may I not attain perfect
> enlightenment. Excluded, however, are those
> who commit the five gravest offenses and abuse
> the right Dharma.

(Pure Land, p. 243)

Upon making the vows, Bodhisattva Dharmakara cultivated the Six Perfections, (see page 202) practices for a
period of innumerable eons. And ten eons ago, he realized
full enlightenment as Amida Buddha and has resided ever
since in the *Sukhavati* Pure Land located billions of Buddha lands to the west (see Chapt. 10 on Pure Land).

In this sacred story, we find the narrative that makes up
the centerpiece of Jodo-Shinshu teaching. Its importance
becomes clear when we see that the central object of
reverence in the shrine is Amida Buddha, not Shakyamuni
Buddha.

2. Circa 200 C.E.:Nagarjuna Shows the Difference between the Easy Path and the Difficult Path.

---

38 I have taken a different reading of this passage than that of Prof.
    Inagaki ("... and call my Name even ten times ...) since I believe
    it reflects the original intent.

Nagarjuna is known as the father of Mahayana philosophy. He has been held in high esteem by many schools of Buddhism. At least eight Japanese schools claim him as their founder. According to legend, he was invited to the underwater world of the Nagas (mythical serpents) where the Naga King gave him some Mahayana scriptures. These scriptures contained teachings that were taught by Shakyamuni Buddha seven hundred years earlier, but had remained hidden ever since. Such is one account of the beginnings of the Mahayana teachings (The Larger Vehicle).

Despite his high status, Nagarjuna, in his younger years before he became a Buddhist, sometimes got himself into trouble. One story tells how he and three of his close friends sneaked into the women's quarters of the royal palace to seduce the women. They also wanted to test their magical skill by making themselves invisible. They quickly learned their magical abilities failed miserably. Nagarjuna managed to escape, but the other three were killed by the guards. Though he escaped unharmed, the experience had a deep impact on him. He began to understand that selfish desire is the root of suffering and magical feats are useless. This understanding helped Nagarjuna to turn to the Buddhist path.

Among his many writings, the one most important for Jodo-Shinshu gives us a metaphor showing the difference between the "easy" Pure Land path and the more "difficult" path.

Although there are numerous ways in the teachings of the Buddha, there are the difficult way and the easy way, as we see in the world. The difficult way is like walking on foot, the easy way is like traveling in a boat. The same can be said about the ways of Bodhisattvas. There are those who are striving toward the Stage of Non-Retrogression by means of practicing the austere Six Perfections, and those who are trying to approach the State of Non-Retrogression by the way of Faith.[39]

The path was difficult for it was believed, particularly in India, that three great eons and innumerable rebirths were required before an aspirant could overcome the obstacles to realizing Buddhahood. To overcome the Three Poisons of greed, hatred and ignorance is no easy task even for monks and nuns; thus, how much more so the task for laypersons![40] In our mountain metaphor, the

---

39 This quote appears in the "Chapter on Easy Practice" of a commentary in Chinese on the *Dashabhumika-sutra* attributed to Nagarjuna. This translation (with slight modification to fit our needs) appears in Shinei Shigefuji. *Nembutsu in Shinran and His Teachers: A Comparison* (Toronto: Toronto Buddhist Church, 1980), pp. 4-5.

40 For example, pride (*mana*) is so subtle and deep-seated that Buddhist practitioners regarded it as one of the last mental obstacles to be eliminated. Now, the "easy path" did not claim to reach in this life the same goal (Buddhahood) as the difficult path. Its goal was to reach a level of enlightenement called "the non-retrogressive state" which assured the practitioners of full

difficult path refers to climbing to the top on one's own power, while the easy path leads to the discovery of the ski lift. Shinran Shonin pays tribute to Nagarjuna:

> Proclaiming the unexcelled Mahayana teaching, he would attain the stage of joy and be born in the land of happiness. Nagarjuna clarifies the hardship on the overland path of difficult practice, and leads us to entrust to the pleasure on the waterway of easy practice.
>
> (*Teachings* I, p. 163)

Nagarjuna, thus, cleared the way for laypersons to pursue the path of enlightenment without undergoing the rigors of being monks and nuns. Making enlightenment accessible to laypersons was significant since it was believed that, generally, people needed to be reborn as monks or nuns before they could realize the highest Buddhist goal.

For this contribution, the Jodo-Shinshu shrine has him depicted among the Seven Masters on a scroll located in the far left section. The Seven Masters, selected by Shinran Shonin, are Nagarjuna (in Japanese, Ryuju), Vasubandhu (Tenjin, ca.4th–5th century), T'an-luan (Donran,476–542), Tao-ch'o (Doshaku, 562–645), Shan-tao (Zendo, 613–681), Genshin (942–1017) and Honen (1133–1212). The first two are Indian, the second three Chinese and the last two Japanese.[41]

Buddhahood once they were born in the Pure Land.

3. Circa 650 C.E.: Master Shan-tao or Zendo (613–81) Focuses on the Human Condition.

In a famous parable of the "Two Rivers and White Path," Shan-tao (Zendo, perhaps the preeminent Pure Land Buddhist scholar and practitioner in Chinese history) paints a picture of the problem of being human and the urgent need to seek the Buddhist path. The seekers are urged to awaken to what modern psychology would call the "shadow," that dimension of the self that one would rather ignore. Here is the story:

A lone traveler comes upon a group of bandits and a horde of wild animals. They are symbols of prejudices and attachments that trap him in a life of anxiety and unhappiness. He runs westward to escape from the bandits and the beasts but is stuck when he comes to a bank of two rivers: a river of fire on the north and a river of raging water to the south. The fire represents greed and the water hatred.

He sees a narrow white path of about twenty centimeters across and forty meters long that connects to the other shore on the western bank. The path symbolizes the Pure Land Buddhist teachings. But the path is narrow and the flames of fire and the raging waves would surely

---

41 For further discussion of the Seven Masters, see Inagaki's *Pure Land Sutras* and Bloom's *Shoshinge: The Heart of Shin Buddhism*. For Shinran's appreciation of them, see *Hymns of the Pure Land Masters* of the Shin Buddhist Translation Series (see Bibliography section).

topple him over. As he looks over his shoulders, the bandits and the wild animals are fast approaching him.

He cannot go backwards or forward, or stay where he is. If he takes any of the three options, he is certain to die. This is called the "three certain deaths." There is nothing he can do but await for death; a point of utter despair.

But at this point he hears the voices of the two Buddhas. Shakyamuni Buddha on the east bank urges him to go across without turning back. Amida Buddha on the west bank beckons him to come across without fear or hesitation. Relying on the caring encouragement of the two Buddhas, the traveler confidently takes the decisive step to walk across. He safely reaches the other shore of enlightenment.

This parable is still a popular topic of many sermons in the Jodo-Shinshu temples and among Chinese Pure Land followers. The story calls up deep feelings and gets to the heart of the reasons for spiritual quests. When Jodo-Shinshu Buddhists talk about their foolish, ego-centered nature, they echo the insight Shan-tao experienced fourteen hundred years ago. This self assessment is not forced on them by religious authority, but is the result of personal experience of their human nature.

The parable does not simply end with the problem but offers a simple solution: recite the Name of Amida while trusting in the Power of Amida's Vow. The simple solution opens this path to even the least refined seekers among the masses. Master Shan-tao spread this message of universal and speedy enlightenment through his writing, artistic works, and public speaking in and around the capital of Ch'ang-an.

While Master Shan-tao's importance in the Chinese Pure Land tradition is undeniable, his role in the Japanese Pure Land development is even more significant. It was his writings that inspired Honen Shonin, Shinran's teacher, to convert to the Pure Land path. He is, thus, duly recognized as the fifth Master of the Jodo-Shinshu transmission lineage and is depicted in the shrine among the Seven Masters.

4. Year 1175: Honen Shonin (1133–1212) Proclaims Independent Status.

Up until Honen's time, Pure Land doctrine and practices in Japan, and in China, had not made up an independent school. Pure Land practices were among many sets of practices carried out under "one roof" of a given temple or school. Honen's independence from the Tendai school in 1175 marked the beginning of the first independent and exclusively Pure Land school in the long history of Buddhism.

Honen had struck a responsive chord, especially among the masses who had been ignored by the older schools whose biggest supporters were the imperial court, aristocrats, and privileged classes. Honen was a reformer and his success in gaining followers made the older Buddhist schools nervous. The older schools became especially angry when the Pure Land school challenged the idea that only the emperor could officially establish a school.

In 1204, the Tendai school petitioned the emperor to restrict the new movement. The next year the powerful Kofukuji Temple in Nara made the same request. They accused Honen's movement of neglecting Shakyamuni Buddha, rejecting the Shinto gods,[42] breaking precepts (of eating meat and gambling), and causing disorder in the nation. These pressures, combined with alleged wrongdoing by some of Honen's key disciples, led to a ban in 1207. A short time later Honen and his top disciples were exiled to remote provinces.

Despite these attempts to block Honen's group, the old schools were not able to stem the tide of the new movement. The new message was a welcome break from the old elitist teachings. The new teaching was caring and simple. The Pure Land teachings were now open to all people regardless of social class, education, wealth, and spiritual abilities. Honen's teaching would even embrace people whose work made them violate precepts, such as fishermen and the emerging Samurai warrior class who had to routinely break the first precept of not killing.

All the followers had to do was simply recite the Name of Amida with faith in the compassionate vow. Honen was convinced his was the best teaching in the Last Age of Dharma (*mappo*), which was believed to have begun

---

42 It may seem odd that any Buddhist group would be offended by another Buddhist group's rejection of the gods of a non-Buddhist religion. But, acceptance of the Shinto gods helped Buddhist sects to prosper and maintain harmony with the civil authorities.

around 1152. After Honen's death in 1212, his disciples, including Shinran, took the message to all corners of Japan.

As the seventh master of the Jodo-Shinshu lineage, Honen is depicted in the shrine with the other six masters. When Shinran spoke of "Jodo-Shinshu" or the "true essence of Pure Land Buddhism," he always had Honen's teachings in mind.

5. Year 1277: Shinran's Daughter Kakushinni (1224–83) Donates her Property to the Order.

When Shinran Shonin died in 1263, he was almost unknown in the Buddhist circles in the capital, Kyoto. He certainly never reached the stature of his teacher Honen. His followers were mostly located 400 miles away from the capital in what is now the Tokyo area, and they were of little political or social importance on the national scene.

But the Jodo-Shinshu road toward its later stature as one of the largest and most powerful Buddhist schools started with the actions taken by Shinran Shonin's youngest daughter, Kakushinni.

After her father's death, Kakushinni built a small family temple with an image of her father on the Otani grounds which she owned. Kakushinni wanted her father's teaching to live on forever so, in 1277 she donated the Otani property and the temple to the Jodo-Shinshu Order. This was a significant move on her part as her father's legacy and teaching would reach more people. The Order, which was made up mostly of her father's faithful from the distant Tokyo area, asked Kakushinni to serve as the Guardian of the Mausoleum who would take care of the property and the temple. Some fifty years later, this mausoleum became an officially recognized temple named the "Honganji" or the Temple of the Original Vow.

Such were the humble beginnings of the Honganji branch of the Jodo-Shinshu school. What is interesting is the key role played by a woman, without whose foresight the Jodo-Shinshu might never have reached its later glory and influence! While Kakushinni is not directly represented in the shrine, her legacy lives on today in the name "Honganji" (Temple of Original Vow) which refers to two of the largest branches of Jodo-Shinshu (See Appendix IV). The Honganji branches evolved from the time of Kakushinni's grandson, Kaku'nyo (1270–1351, the third Abbot), to take on a primogeniture system, that is to say, the position of the Abbot or Monshu (Gate-Head) came to be handed down to the oldest male heir. The present Monshu Sokunyo (1945–) is the twenty-fourth in line.

6. Year 1465: Rennyo Shonin (1415–1499) Escapes Destruction of the Honganji Temple.

Although there had been rumors of an attack, Rennyo and his followers were not ready for the swift onslaught of the monks from Mt. Hiei. When about one hundred and fifty monk-soldiers from Hiei arrived at the modest Honganji Temple, they quickly broke in and overwhelmed the small number of guards. Rennyo's attendants helped him escape alive, and he took cover in a friendly temple. By the time support from the nearby areas rushed to their aid, the temple had been plundered and destroyed beyond repair.

Rennyo Shonin, the eighth Abbot of the Honganji (before its split into Nishi or western and Higashi or eastern branches), is known as the "restorer" or "the second founder" of Jodo-Shinshu. He earned this title by building the young Shinshu order into one of the best known Buddhist schools in his lifetime. The great things he did are more surprising when we think about the personal hardships he lived with as a child. His mother left him when he was six years old, and he was forced to live with a stepmother who didn't like him. His family was so poor that he often went without eating for two or three days. Still, he had good religious training. He had some formal training, and he went with his father to visit Honganji supporters in the faraway districts.

When the Otani Honganji (temple) was destroyed, Rennyo lost both his place of birth and his home of over fifty years. More importantly, it had become the spiritual home of a growing Shinshu community. Rennyo had built a large group of followers during the seven years after assuming the role of Abbot at the age of forty-three. It was this success that had caused some Tendai temples to be alarmed and jealous. When they saw Rennyo as a big enough threat, they attacked his temple. Rennyo's problems had just begun. His enemies kept harassing his rag-tag group until Rennyo fled from the area.

We see an image of Rennyo and his family and supporters fleeing their temporary homes by night carrying whatever they could on their backs. These attacks by fellow Buddhist schools strike us as un-Buddhist-like behavior, but they show us the mood of the time. Japan had entered a time of political unrest and warfare that flooded the nation.

The hard times of his younger years had made Rennyo tough. He fought against his troubles and turned problems into opportunities for growth. He moved his headquarters to Yoshizaki, on the Japan Sea side, where he again built up a large Shinshu following. Without the strong national government, the nation was in the throes of political disunity and civil wars. As the local conflicts spread, Rennyo had to steer a careful course and control his followers. Some of the followers played important roles in the battles among the vying provincial warrior lords as well as between these lords and their peasants claiming greater autonomy.

Having built a strong center for the Honganji, Rennyo returned to Kyoto. At the age of sixty-eight, he built the temple at Yamashina which became the center of the Honganji Order. With a temple from which to work, Rennyo was able to teach and spread the teachings. At seventy-five, Rennyo gave up his post as Abbot to his fifth son, Jitsunyo, but he kept working after retirement. At the ripe age of eighty-two, he established the Ishiyama Temple in the city of Osaka.

Rennyo's skill in rebuilding the Honganji (both the main temple and the entire network of Honganji branch temples) is truly remarkable. He had a total of twenty-seven children from five wives (not concurrently) with the last child born to him at the age of eighty-four! He led the Honganji Branch through a tough time with strength, courage, and vision. Rennyo's contribution still shows today in many parts of the tradition.

As the result of his status as the Restorer or the Second Founder, Rennyo is given a special place in the shrine. He is "housed" in a manner virtually equal to Shinran, but on the opposite side (left) of Amida Buddha.

7. Year 1570: Warlord Oda Nobunaga Attacks Ishiyama Honganji.

Political turmoil and fighting grew worse all through Japan during the sixteenth century. The Honganji again fell victim to the conflict when a feudal lord attacked the thriving Yamashina Honganji and burned it to the ground. Abbot Shonyo, his family, and followers barely escaped and found refuge at Ishiyama Temple in Osaka one hundred miles away.

In its new home, the Honganji branch began to thrive again and grow in influence and membership despite the turmoil around them. The fighting finally dragged them in. The most powerful warlord, Oda Nobunaga, intended to bring the whole country under his control. He wanted Ishiyama Honganji because it was an important military location. Nobunaga was also uneasy about the great power and influence of the Buddhist schools, especially the Honganji. They could be a threat to his dream of becoming the *Shogun*, the Supreme Commander.

In 1570, Nobunaga ordered Abbot Kennyo and his followers out of Ishiyama. Kennyo bluntly refused. This started a ten year battle between the two forces. Kennyo saw Nobunaga as the "enemy of the Buddha-Dharma" who would stop at nothing until he gained control of the entire country. Nobunaga was sympathetic to Christianity, which also bothered Kennyo.

When Nobunaga started his siege in September of 1570, Abbot Kennyo appealed to the Honganji Shinshu followers and sympathetic feudal lords throughout Japan. The response was sensational. Men and supplies poured in to defend the mother temple. Though outnumbered and less experienced, the Honganji defenders repulsed a series of attacks by the mighty Nobunaga army. They were inspired by the belief that they were defending their faith from the enemy of Buddhism. With the combination of religious inspiration and material support by the large network of supporters, the Honganji managed to fight the Nobunaga forces for the next ten years!

But by 1580, Nobunaga controlled much of central Japan and had isolated the Honganji from its supporters. Abbot Kennyo, fearing the total massacre of his people, agreed to leave Ishiyama. His oldest son, Kyo'nyo, and his supporters, refused to concede. This was the background for the split of the Honganji into Nishi (West) and Higashi (East) branches. Kennyo chose his second son, Junnyo, as his successor. His line developed into Nishi Honganji, while the first son Kyo'nyo went on to establish the Higashi Honganji (or Otani Branch).[43]

Although the Honganji was driven from Ishiyama and split into two branches, the Shinshu institutions far outlived the apparent victor, Nobunaga. He was assassinated by his general just two years later in 1582. The memory of the warlord would soon fade, but the Honganji would keep the lamp of Dharma burning for centuries afterwards.

The Buddhist Churches of America, Honpa Hongwanji Mission of Hawaii and Buddhist Churches of Canada belong to the Nishi Honganji, not to Higashi Honganji which is less well represented in North America. This affiliation has its roots all the way back to the Ishiyama conflict over four hundred years ago.

8. Year 1806: Government Renders Verdict on Sango-wakuran Controversy.

The modern idea of keeping politics separate from religion did not exist during the Tokugawa period (1602–1867). The government used the Buddhist temples as government outposts where the people's official records were kept. The Buddhist schools were banned from preaching the Dharma to convert new followers. All members of the same family were required to belong to the same school.[44] What is more, priests were discour-

---

43   See Appendix IV for explanation of these two and other eight branches of Jodo-Shinshu.

44   This, in my view, has contributed to the practice even today of regarding religious participation in terms of family and not of individuals. For example, adults with their own households tend

aged from suggesting any new ideas that were not already in the tradition.

A major argument about doctrine broke out among the scholars of Nishi Honganji at the end of the 1700s. On one side stood the professors of the Academy (the highest center of sectarian learning) in Kyoto and on the other side were the scholars in the remote areas. The Academy professors wanted to emphasize the dynamic dimension of "Shinjin awareness" as manifested in one's daily activities. They thought it was important to express one's spiritual understanding in the way we act, speak, and think. The technical name for this is "the three karmic actions" (*sango*) of mind, body, and speech. The scholars from the outlying areas, on the other hand, argued that the serene mind of Shinjin awareness is central to the life of the person of Shinjin awareness. In their view, the three karmic actions become uncomfortably close to being self-power practice (see page 102). The clash can be seen as a difference between a more active and outward interpretation versus a more passive and inward emphasis.

While arguments about doctrine were nothing new to the Shinshu tradition, what draws our attention to this dispute is how much the government controlled and

---

not to become temple members as long as their parents are members, and family memorial services continue to be the primary form of contact with the temple for many Jodo-Shinshu Buddhists.

interfered in the affairs of religious institutions. The government in the Tokugawa period was very much against any kind of change. It is not surprising, then, that the government courts finally brought an end to the argument in 1806 by deciding against any change in the doctrine. The winning side in this case happened to be the more passive definition favored by the scholars in the outlying areas. This decision was largely based on a simple rule: Accept the old and reject the new! Chido, the head scholar of the Academy at the time, not only lost the case but faced a punishment of exile to a distant island. But because he had died in prison before the verdict was handed down, it is reported that his ashes were sent to the island in his place!

The dispute and the way it was solved had a strong impact on the way the teachings would be understood. Today, the passive definition is dominant in the Nishi Honganji teachings. The emphasis is on the activities of Amida Buddha over those of the human seeker. There is little stress on the active definition of Shinjin whose advocates lost out in the government decision of 1806.

9. Year 1899: First Missionaries Arrive in San Francisco.

When the first two missionaries of the Nishi Honganji arrived on September 1, 1899, they were interviewed by reporters of the *San Francisco Chronicle*. Two weeks later, their picture appeared with the following caption:

> Dr. Shuye Sonoda and Rev. Kakuryo Nishi-
> jima, two Buddhist priests who are the sons of
> Buddhist priests of Japan, have come here to
> establish a Buddhist mission at 807 Polk Street
> and to convert Japanese and later Americans to
> the ancient Buddhist faith. They will teach that
> God is not the creator, but the created, not a
> real existence, but a figment of the human
> imagination, and that pure Buddhism is a bet-
> ter moral guide than Christianity.
>
> Their priestly robes are as interesting as the
> lesson that they would present. As they posed
> before the camera in the hallway near their
> rooms in the Occidental Hotel yesterday, they
> were the wonderment of all the Japanese em-
> ployees who could assemble for the glimpse of
> the sacred garb.

These first missionaries were not received with open arms when they came to America. For example, notice how the *Chronicle* comments that, "They will teach that . . . pure Buddhism is a better moral guide than Christianity." One cannot help but sense a combative tone in that comment.

Some people in the Japanese community didn't give them much of a welcome, either. The groundwork for the official missionaries was laid several years earlier. One year before they came, a Buddhist representative met with the Japanese Consul, but records show he did not like the idea of bringing Buddhism to this country. He feared that bringing a "foreign religion" here would cause problems when Japan and America were at peace. The Consul was upset by the idea and asked whether the American government would allow a foreign religion to come in. He saw Buddhism as a threat to peace![45]

Despite the uncaring attitude, even among some of the leaders of the Japanese community on the west coast, the members of the Buddhist community in San Francisco pressed hard for their dream. On September 1, 1898, (exactly one year before the arrival of the first missionaries), the members of the Young Men's Buddhist Association met to draft a petition to the Nishi Honganji headquarters. The petition was signed by eighty-three people and asked the Honganji to start a center headed by Buddhist priests sent from their homeland. Surrounded by a lonely, unfriendly religious world, their strong wishes were expressed with the following words from their petition:

> In the eight directions are non-Buddhist forces surrounding the Japanese Buddhists, and we cannot be at ease. It is as if we are sitting on the point of a pin; no matter how we move, we will be pricked. Our burning desire to hear the Teachings (of the Buddha) is about to explode from every pore in our bodies.[46]

---

45 Tetsuden Kashima. *Buddhism in America: The Social Organization of an Ethnic Institution* (Westport, Connecticut: Greenwood Press, 1977), p. 14. Much of this section is based on this book.

From this humble beginning, in just fifteen years the group grew to twenty-five churches and branches. In 1914, the first general meeting of the ministers and lay representatives gathered to officially form the North American Buddhist Mission. In the following year, it sponsored the World Buddhist Conference during the Panama Canal Exposition held in San Francisco. In the 1920s and 1930s, the number of churches and members kept growing, due mostly to the increased discrimination against the Japanese by the general American public. The crescendo of anti-Japanese sentiments culminated in the 1924 Alien Land Laws and the Oriental Exclusion Act. According to the new laws, Japanese nationals could no longer own property, and new immigration from Japan was terminated. The Exclusion Act ironically turned out to be a windfall for the Buddhist temples.

The Japanese community interpreted the law as extremely unjust. Many of them, including those who were undecided, became members of Buddhist temples. The Buddhist temples came to be perceived as an ethnic refuge and bastion for Japanese culture amidst the sea of hostile society. This is reflected in an observation made during that period about the Gardena Buddhist Church:

> After the passage of the Immigration Law of 1924 discriminating against the Japanese, the number of Buddhists increased rapidly, and

---

46   *Ibid.*, p. 15.

so did that of the Buddhist churches. Before that event, some of them had been hesitant in declaring themselves Buddhists, considering such an act impudent in a Christian country. But the immigration law made them more defiant and bold in asserting what they believed to be their rights; it made them realize the necessity of cooperation for the sake of their own security and welfare, and naturally they sought centers of their communal activity in their Buddhist churches.[47]

The Buddhist Churches of America (B.C.A.) has designated September 1st as Founding Day, and it is observed by its affiliated temples.

10. Year 1944: Regrouping of Jodo-Shinshu During World War II

May the injustices and humiliation suffered here as a result of hysteria, racism and economic exploitation never emerge again.

These sad and hopeful words are etched on a plaque at Manzanar, California, one of the ten concentration camps set up by the United States Government during World

---

47   Kosei Ogura, "A Sociological Study of the Buddhist Churches in North America, With a Case Study of Gardena, California, Congregation." Master's Thesis, Univ. of Southern California,: 1932, pp. 85-86.

War II. The camps were both home and prison to 110,000 Japanese Americans and their immigrant parents, after they were forced out of their own homes in states on the west coast. These American citizens and legal residents were locked up without due process of law. This happened because the war made some people afraid of them. Others hated them because of their race, and still others wanted to make money by stealing their property. It took almost half a century for the government to finally issue a formal apology to the internees, and to agree that the internment was one of the most shameful chapters in American history.

Among the first to be rounded up in the early days of the war were the Buddhist priests. Mrs. Shinobu Matsuura's husband was the Rev. Issei Matsuura. He was the minister of a temple in Guadalupe, a small farming community in central coastal California. Mrs. Matsuura, a highly respected spiritual and community leader in her own right, later recalled those terrifying events in her book, *Higan* (Compassionate Vow).[48]

---

48   I find Mrs. Matsuura's contribution to the development of Jodo-Shinshu in North America to be enormous. Not only did she run a children's home in the central coastal California town of Guadalupe for many years prior to World War II, but also nurtured the start of the Buddhist Study Center in Berkeley which in the 1950s attracted numerous scholars and intellectuals to study Buddhism. The Center developed into what is presently the Institute of Buddhist Studies. I recall with distinct memory her utter dedication and a profound personal appreciation and understanding of the Nembutsu teaching. She had given

February 18, 1942, early morning, still in our night clothes and huddled by the heater, we listened grimly to the news over the radio. There was a loud rapping on the back door. Three men stood there. They were the FBI.

"We came to arrest Rev. Matsuura," said one, as they came through the door. I had a foreboding that something like this would happen. But when the time actually came, I felt crushed. I was instructed to pack a change of clothing for my husband. Hurriedly, I put his underwear and toiletries in a bag. Separately, I wrapped his *koromo* (priest robes) and *kesa* (a miniature version of the original monastic robe that is worn around the neck), *seiten* (book of sacred writings) and *Kanmuryojukyo sutra* (the *Contemplation Sutra*).

"Only bare necessities," they said, but he being a minister, the extra religious articles were allowed. My husband walked the long corridor to the *hondo* (Buddha hall), lit the candle and incense and quietly read the *Tanbutsuge (sutra)*. Our youngest daughter, Kiyo, and I bowed in *gassho* (placing the palms together as an expression of reverence), realizing this

---

Dharma talks at every one of the 60 or so B.C.A. temples and in many other Jodo-Shinshu temples in Canada, Hawaii and Japan.

may be our last parting. The FBI stood at attention through the sutra chanting.

In April 1942, Mrs. Matsuura was evacuated to the camps, along with the entire Japanese American community. She would later write:

> Whatever land and property were acquired in the almost fifty years of immigrant history leading up to that day were to be sold at any price or just abandoned. We were told to leave with only what we could carry. Bearing numbered tags identifying us as "enemy aliens," and steeped in uncertainty, we tearfully left our home.

The camps had been hastily built in desolate areas across the western states. Once there, the internees found they were surrounded by barbed wire fences and armed guards. Sixty percent of the internees were Buddhists, mostly of the Jodo-Shinshu school. Though they were locked up, they still practiced their religion. Sunday morning services were well attended. For many, the services helped them to deal with their deep feelings of betrayal and the uncertainties about their own well-being.

Ironically, the most critical step in the Americanization of Jodo-Shinshu Buddhism took place in the concentration camps located in Topaz, Utah. The organization had been controlled by priests who were almost all missionaries from Japan and lay leaders who were first generation immigrants. Japanese was the primary language used in all organization business.

During the internment, the American-born second generation began to exercise more influence. The great change started with a series of meetings at the Topaz camp in early 1944, and climaxed with a conference in Salt Lake City (east of the quarantined zone) in July of that year. A new constitution was adopted that called for a shift to English as the primary language and a new name: The Buddhist Churches of America. The conference also marked another important change — the growing power of the lay members in relation to the priests, whose authority and influence had been enormous in the prewar years.

The change in the name from North American Buddhist Mission to Buddhist Churches of America was the direct result of the 1944 meeting. This move was part of a serious effort to plant the roots of Jodo-Shinshu in the new American soil.

What do you see as the greatest challenge facing the Jodo-Shinshu institutions in North America?

The temples need to become fully Dharma-centered. In the past, Dharma has had to share its position with the cultural (ethnicity, arts, social, etc.) needs of the Japanese American members for the historical reasons discussed above. If the cultural elements continue to dominate the center, the temple will exclude people who are interested in Buddhism but do not share the same strong interests in cultural matters. The universal nature of the Dharma, in contrast, has the ability to include diverse groups and to give spiritual meaning to their interests. Dharma can then function as the "hub" of the many cultural activities of the temple. The cultural activities will not disappear any time soon, nor do we want them to, but they need to "step down" to take their secondary place in the life of a temple.

Do you think the challenge will be met successfully?

I am optimistic. I believe that we are in an ideal environment for the teaching to stand on its own. As we discussed above, Jodo-Shinshu suffered a great deal of persecution and control by the government throughout much of its history in Japan. This suppression, however, is unlikely to happen in North America with its ideals of the separation of state and religion. Further, North Americans generally turn to teachings as the foundation of their personal values and action to a greater degree than their modern counterparts in Japan. With this religious environment, Buddhism has already attracted the serious interest of many seekers, particularly those who feel disillusioned by organized Western religions. I believe that when the Jodo-Shinshu teachings are correctly understood, they have all the potential to successfully meet the needs of many North Americans.

Chapter Six

The Jodo-Shinshu Path: Simple Yet Not Easy

Why is Jodo-Shinshu not more well-known in North America?

It is curious that a religion that has existed in North America for close to one hundred years is not better known. I think the reasons have to do with not enough push and pull.

First, the push: It's partly because the Jodo-Shinshu Buddhists have not actively pushed the message out. I believe numerous cultural and historical factors contribute to this. The strict governmental control and persecution of the tradition throughout its history in Japan (as we saw earlier in Chapt. 5) has created an atmosphere of caution and left the tradition with very little experience in propagation. And these historical factors reinforced what I believe are two of the dominant characteristics of Japanese social organizations: hierarchy and group loyalty.[49]

And of course, the Japanese American experience of severe discrimination that culminated in the Second World War internment experience (see page 93) contributed to the temples being social and cultural centers to an even greater degree than the churches of other immigrant groups to America. The members of the Buddhist temples were forced to "circle their wagons" and turn inward.

Second, the pull: Even when the teaching is presented, those interested in Buddhism in the West seem more pulled to the other forms of Buddhism because of four factors.

What are these four factors that you see?

They are 1) absence of meditation, 2) no superstitious beliefs or worldly benefits, 3) non-monastic priesthood, and 4) superficial similarities with Christianity.

Can you explain what you mean by, "Absence of meditation"?

Jodo-Shinshu does not *require* meditation like most other schools of Buddhism. When there is a set practice that is required of everyone, the seekers feel secure. They like knowing clearly what to do and seeing signs of

---

49 Hierarchical relationships within an organization tend to discourage grass roots innovations and initiative in favor of directives from the top which are generally conservative in nature. Group loyalty feeds on the assumption of a clear distinction between insiders and outsiders, discouraging a more fluid interaction and association with members of other groups.

progress. This is especially true of those who left the Jewish and Christian traditions. They are eager to "do" something. Many are particularly attracted to meditation because it is "therapeutic" and, most of all, concrete.

This explains the popularity of Zen, Tibetan, and Theravada forms of Buddhism. Even some Christians, particularly Catholic priests, are integrating Buddhist meditation into their daily regimen. I believe that the popularity of Buddhism in North America is due in large measure to the availability of its highly developed and easily-accessible meditative practices. To use an analogy, if we are like the circus tightrope walkers, then meditation provides us with the technique of how to walk and the pole to balance ourselves. In contrast, Jodo-Shinshu lends little assistance on the "how" of walking but simply says "Don't worry, there is a safety net in case you fall!" With that assurance, we are able to be ourselves and walk naturally across.

Then there is no practice in Jodo-Shinshu?

We need to first define what we mean by practice. In my view, there are two meanings of practice. One is to cultivate and change one's nature, especially to *eradicate* greed, hatred and delusion. This demands utmost dedication which essentially only the monks and nuns can satisfactorily carry out. The second meaning, however, does not call for such extreme change in nature but fosters self-reflection, trust and a new awareness about oneself and the world. Shinran Shonin rejected the first type of practice, calling it "self-power" (*jiriki*) that belongs to the "gate to the path of the sages" (*shodo-mon*).

> Self-power is the effort to attain birth, …by endeavoring to make yourself worthy through amending the confusion in your acts, words, and thoughts, confident of your own powers and guided by your own calculation. Other Power is the entrusting of yourself to the 18th among Amida Tathagata's Vows, the Primal Vow of birth through nembutsu, which Amida selected from among all other practices.
>
> (*Letters*, pp. 22-23)

Why did Shinran Shonin reject the first type of practice?

There are a number of reasons. The first and foremost is that enlightenment is already here and now, right under our feet. Do you recall the sailor in the metaphor? He awakened to the fact that he is safe and sound right where he was, in the middle of the ocean. Simply by a shift in his awareness, he found himself embraced by a supporting ocean. This awakening did not require him to swim to the distant island to find safety. The ocean was safe all along; the sailor simply needed to awaken to that truth. The ocean is that "Other Power" about which Shinran Shonin speaks so often.

Shinran Shonin's rejection of the first type of practice also stemmed from his fear that such practices often led to attachment and self-righteousness. He felt that often practice increased the very problem it set out to overcome, self-centeredness. We all know of "religious" people who carry themselves with an air of self-righteous and superior attitude because they, and only they, are practicing correctly. There is, however, also the danger of going the opposite extreme of becoming too lazy and complacent, to which Jodo-Shinshu was especially vulnerable throughout its history.[50]

Shinran Shonin chose the second type of practice, right? What form does it take in Jodo-Shinshu?

It has primarily taken the form of "listening to the Dharma" (*monpo*). We listen to the Dharma by seriously and intently listening to the Dharma talks given by teachers and, in a broader sense of the word, by studying the traditional scriptures and writings of contemporary teachers. Through intense and sincere listening, we are transformed to internalize the Buddhist ideals. This internalization allows us to practice the teachings in daily life, in general accordance with the aims of precepts and meditations of the other Buddhist schools. I call these "self-effort," as distinguished from "self-power." Self-effort is vital and needed. It is "practicing" without the self-centered motivation and attitudes of self-power!

Actually, so long as one does not see his efforts as directly causing enlightenment, a Jodo-Shinshu Buddhist is free to engage in any of the well-known forms of practice, including Zen and Vipasanna (of Theravada) meditations. Jodo-Shinshu strongly rejects the idea that

---

50 Some misguided followers thought that the "Other Power" teaching meant that they did not have to do anything. Others went so far as to purposely commit evil in order to qualify as beneficiaries of Amida's compassionate Vow.

our actions *in themselves* cause our enlightenment. When Jodo-Shinshu Buddhists practice, we do it out of a sense of gratitude. The late Prof. Ryukyo Fujimoto, a widely respected teacher of many active Jodo-Shinshu priests in North America, spoke of gratitude:

> Birth through Faith alone, as based on the EighteenthVow, *does not by any means discourage other Buddhist practices.* They must, however, be performed *in a spirit of gratitude* toward the Tathagata (Amida Buddha)... (emphases added)[51]

When we act out of deep-felt gratitude, we become less self-centered.

I appreciate the freedom of the idea that you can do what you want as long as you do it with the proper attitude. What I wish to know is what do you do when Jodo-Shinshu Buddhists get together?

In our services, we have chanting, singing, pledges and quiet reflection, all centered around the Dharma talk usually delivered by a priest. Among all of these, I feel that chanting comes closest to what non-Buddhists and other Buddhists would regard as practice.

We chant the words of Shakyamuni Buddha in the Pure Land sutras or from the words of Shinran Shonin. We chant to honor and praise their virtues as well as to internalize the meaning of their words. We chant aloud

---

51   Ryukyo Fujimoto, *Shin Buddhism's Essence: The Tannisho*, p. 97.

in unison in the traditional style. Each word is chanted with care in the proper note and intonation. We normally chant anywhere from seven to forty minutes depending on what we are chanting.

What I like about chanting is that it is done together with everyone gathered at the service. Both adults and children chant together. This fosters an intimate sense of connectedness with others, much more so than when we sit in meditation on our own. When we share the same experience through chanting, we develop a positive and trusting attitude toward others and ultimately toward the world. We then become more capable of realizing the caring that we receive in our lives and so become able to identify with the sailor in our metaphor who demonstrated complete trust in the caring ocean.

But chanting is not meditation, is it?

In my view, it serves a very similar function to meditation in Zen, particularly of the Soto line of Zen where sitting meditation does not in and of itself directly cause awakening. Meditation is understood more as an expression of enlightenment. The same can be said of chanting and particularly of Nembutsu (the utterance of the Name of Amida, *Namo Amida Butsu*).[52] Zen and Pure Land have much more in common than normally thought. Some of my American Soto Zen practitioner friends now

---

52 Persons of Shinjin awareness utter the Name throughout the course of their daily lives as expression of gratitude to the Buddha for their transformed lives.

openly acknowledge the affinity between the two traditions. In my view, the difference can be seen not in terms of meditation versus devotion but in the emphasis among the three traditional Buddhist actions: bodily, oral and mental. Zen meditation stresses the bodily action, while Jodo-Shinshu stresses the oral action.[53] Both traditions aim to transform the mental.

Chanting similarly requires discipline and focus in order to be carried out properly. More importantly, chanting can also lead to a quieting of the mind. This was clearly brought home to me when I observed a group of fourteen Buddhist monks and one priest during an annual celebration of the Buddha's birthday. They sat on the stage through the long hour-and-a-half ceremony. The monks exhibited calm and mindfulness as expected, but I could not help but be impressed by the one priest who was equally, if not more, calm and mindful in his actions. And that priest was Rev. Haruyoshi Kusada, a teacher of chanting in the Jodo-Shinshu tradition!

How about the second factor, "No superstitious beliefs or worldly benefits"?

Jodo-Shinshu firmly rejects any use of its teachings to gain worldly or secular benefits. The Jodo-Shinshu Preamble says, "We shall not conduct petitionary prayers for secular benefits or magical acts, and shall not rely on

---

53   This of course does not apply to all Buddhist meditations, which lead to deeper levels of mental concentration (*samadhi*) that cannot be realized by chanting or *Nembutsu*.

fortune telling and other superstitious acts." This lasting dislike for such acts supports Shinran Shonin's stance against using religion to gain worldly benefits.

In contrast, there are many temples of other schools in Japan today that actively foster benefits. Any foreign visitor can easily see the fortune papers tied to tree branches seeking everything from success in university entrance exams to household prosperity, longevity, and protection from fire. Temple visitors often direct incense smoke with their hands onto the parts of the body that are giving them aches and pains. That the favorite spot for this "smoke blessing" is the top of the head shows the high value of brain power in the competitive Japanese society.

These requests are certainly not evil in the secular sense, but they go against the Buddhist principle (Second Noble Truth) that desire is the cause of suffering. Shinran Shonin was, thus, strongly against such practices. Certainly, a religious organization can gain more followers by agreeing with and using these desires. We saw how well it works in the examples I gave from Japan.

What do you mean by "non-monastic priesthood?"

Most North Americans who turn to Eastern religions, including Buddhism, look to charismatic spiritual teachers who are monks or nuns. The Dalai Lama of the Tibetan tradition is the best example of this kind of teacher. Zen and Theravada teachers also fit this ideal image. Many find their shaven heads and flowing robes attractive.

In contrast, the Jodo-Shinshu priests look like ordinary people. In most cases, their heads are not shaved and in North America, men wear neckties and suits. They wear their religious robes only for ceremonial services. You might see male priests baby-sitting their infant children while working around the temple. They are a far cry from the common Western image of a Buddhist teacher!

Plus, the Shinshu Sangha is often referred to as a community of Fellow Seekers and Fellow Travelers (*ondobo ondogyo*). In this relationship, though the priests may be at the head of the group, they are nevertheless traveling together toward the common goal. The priests are not agents or representatives of Amida Buddha nor are they regarded as *gurus* (here "guru" refers to an attitude and not to any clergy of other Buddhist schools) who hold absolute authority over the spiritual lives of the members. In fact, the tradition has been extremely careful not to foster "guru worship" of any kind and has worked hard particularly in North America to apply democratic ideals to matters related to the role of priests. This view is reflected in Shinran Shonin's self image as "neither monk nor lay."

What do you mean by the fourth factor, "superficial similarities to Christianity"?

Although there are fundamental differences between the teachings of Jodo-Shinshu and Christianity, many, at first glance, find some similarities between the two traditions. In my view, the similarities are found in the areas of 1) human nature, 2) the ultimate, and 3) the source of spiritual resolution.

With regard to human nature, Christians regard humans as deeply sinful[54] while Jodo-Shinshu regard humans as foolish (*bombu*). (See "foolish being") Both religions see human nature as self-centered, and assert that people are unable to change their nature fundamentally through *their own efforts*.

The ultimate in Christianity is God, while it is Amida Buddha in Jodo-Shinshu. Both God and Amida represent spiritual power that lies outside our human capabilities. Both also have qualities that are diametrically opposed to the "sinful" Christians and "foolish" Jodo-Shinshu Buddhists.

Both teachings find humans to be incapable of realizing the spiritual goal by pulling themselves up by their own bootstraps. Because of our sinful and foolish nature respectively, nothing we do can liberate us. So, no works or disciplines are required. Instead, our spiritual resolution relies on power beyond the self: God's grace in Christianity[55] and the Other Power in Jodo-Shinshu.

---

54 I am aware that there has been a tendency among many mainline Christian denominations to de-emphasize the notion of original sin and sin in general. However, the doctrine of sin is much too central to the Christian faith to be readily erased, and this trend to de-emphasize sin is not shared by other Christians, especially those of the conservative branches.

55 Pelagius believed in the human capability to lead moral life, but he was severely criticized by Augustine (354–430 C.E.) who argued that moral life was not possible without God's grace. Augustine's position won out and has ever since comprised the core doctrine of Christianity in the West

Wouldn't these similarities encourage people to examine Jodo-Shinshu more carefully?

That is not necessarily true. In fact, those from a Western religious background seeking new forms of religion are often not attracted by qualities similar to their own faiths. They seek the fresh, novel, and exotic. If they see just the surface, Jodo-Shinshu often does not have enough separation from what they left behind.

Are these similarities superficial?

Yes. I believe if they looked deeper, they would find that these Jodo-Shinshu teachings are rooted in basic Buddhism. So, they differ in subtle yet fundamental ways from the similar teachings in Christian thought. To do justice to them, I will elaborate on each of the three points later (see Chaps. 7, 8 and 9). Permit me, however, to say a few words in general.

With regard to human imperfection, sin implies a failure to keep one's promise with God by not living in accordance with his will. The focus is on one's relationship to God. In contrast, foolishness (*bombu*) in Jodo-Shinshu stems from being awakened by the Buddha's wisdom. The focus is the realization of one's inability to overcome one's self-centered attachments through one's own power. So, they differ in the reasons why humans are believed to be imperfect.

Secondly, there is a definite difference in the way we think of the ultimate. God is a supernatural being who is the Maker, Lord and Father. Amida has none of the same characteristics, but is the "spiritual power" that we experience as understanding and caring in our lives.

Thirdly, there is a subtle difference in the way we relate to the transcendent spiritual source. Christians maintain an ongoing personal relationship with God who exists independently from humans and the world. This relationship is maintained largely through prayers, sacraments and contemplation. In contrast, Jodo-Shinshu Buddhists do not regard Amida as a divine being with whom they maintain an ongoing relationship. They realize their essential oneness with Amida in the oral recitation, for Amida is none other than the Name *Namo Amida Butsu* (see page 150).

That does help a great deal to clarify the difference, and to show that Jodo-Shinshu is rooted in Buddhism.

Good. As I said, I will elaborate later, which should make the distinctions clearer. Unfortunately, even thinkers and scholars have been too quick to judge Jodo-Shinshu. For example, Dr. Albert Schweitzer in 1936 commented, "Of course the doctrine of Shinran is an outrage on Buddhism."[56] More recently, Professor Heinz Bechert remarked, "It takes the ideas of the Buddha and, in a way, twists them into their opposite. The most radical spokesman for this approach is Shinran Shonin..."[57] Their opinion is due precisely to seeing only the surface; they don't

---

56   Albert Schweitzer. *Indian Thought and Its Development.* Translated by Mrs. Charles E. B. Buswell (1936. Boston: The Beacon Press, 1957), p. 154.

57   Küng, Hans et al. *Christianity and the World Religions* (Maryknoll, NY: Orbis Books, 1986), p. 373.

see that the flower (Jodo-Shinshu) is fully connected to the tree trunk of basic Buddhism.

If the seekers who are dissatisfied with their own faith look deeper, they will find that Jodo-Shinshu offers a "middle path." It has some familiar teachings as we've discussed earlier, plus the appeal of family orientation and the collective and emotional involvement in the religious services. But Jodo-Shinshu also offers freedom from many of the things seekers give as reasons for leaving their original religions: for example, 1) an oppressive sense of guilt, 2) the constant fear of judgment, 3) emphasis on belief and morality, 4) discouragement of questions, 5) rejection of personal experience, 6) belief in an all-knowing, all-powerful God, and 7) the conflict between a loving God and an unhappy world.[58]

Do you see these four factors as a real problem in getting more people to take interest in Jodo-Shinshu?

If people are looking for simple black-and-white answers, these reasons might keep them from taking a serious interest in Jodo-Shinshu. People who are patient and sincerely interested will see beyond these four surface issues.

---

58   These are based on what I have heard from the converts I have known, and thus I am not in any way implying that they are normative qualities in these religions.

What is the relationship between Jodo-Shinshu and other Buddhist teachings?

Jodo-Shinshu is one of the paths to enlightenment. Shinran Shonin felt this was the best path for all Buddhists, especially householder persons who are not monks or nuns. He believed that he lived in the Last Age of Dharma,[59] when the previous paths could no longer effectively lead people of the decadent period to enlightenment.

Are there monks and nuns in Shinshu?

No, Shinshu is a non-monastic movement. Shinran Shonin was a monk until age twenty-nine, but left the order because he found a Buddhist path for everyone. He married, raised a family, and worked hard to spread the teaching to everyone, whether they were monks or lay persons. Shinshu clergy have allowed married priests from the beginning, because it is not deed (precepts or meditation), but outlook (Shinjin awareness) that is most important.

---

59   This is the third period in a progressively deteriorating evolution after the death of Shakyamuni Buddha. The first period, the Age of True Dharma, lasts 500 (or 1,000) years, followed by the Age of Counterfeit Dharma for 1,000 years, with the Last Age of Dharma lasting 10,000 years. According to this theory, the Last Age was believed to have begun in 1152 C.E. In the first period, both the teaching and enlightened persons existed, but in the second period only the teaching could be found; in the Last Age of Dharma even the teaching disappeared, thus calling for the new Pure Land teaching.

I've heard that many people find it hard to understand the Jodo-Shinshu path even though it is called the "easy path." Is that true?

Yes, I agree. Part of the difficulty is that many are looking to religion only for moral guidance instead of spiritual insight. To give you an example, a young mother of a Dharma (Sunday) school student came up to me after my talk to complain:

> The Jodo-Shinshu teaching really stresses the ego, selfishness, and foolishness of human beings. But how about guidance on how to get along in this society with all its complex problems? My child needs confidence, not self-criticism!

Her comments are familiar. I find that attitude expressed in my own religion as well.

I am sure that is true. In a religious institution, there are 1) those who are interested mostly in moral guidance, and 2) those who are interested in spiritual matters. If I were to illustrate this with a triangle, the first group makes up the bottom half, while the second makes up the top half. The first category of members outnumbers the second category in most religious groups.

Moral guidance is a real and valid concern, especially for parents interested in their children's religious education. Jodo-Shinshu must take up this challenge with utmost seriousness if it is to nurture the next generation of confident, committed members. But this moral guidance must be rooted in the spiritual. In Buddhism, the spiritual is primary while the moral dimension is secondary (see p. 183).

This "problem" is not confined to your Jodo-Shinshu religion.

That may be so. In my view, however, Shinshu is especially subject to the criticism because its core doctrine is so narrowly focused on spiritual issues, with only limited concern for ethical and social issues. And all this talk, for example, about "karmic evil" and "ordinary foolish people," which the teaching stresses (and for which Jodo-Shinshu is often criticized by people like the young mother) can only be fully understood within the spiritual context.

In contrast, traditional Jodo-Shinshu doctrine has very little to say about moral guidance and conduct. In Japan, it was primarily the Neo-Confucian values and popular Japanese beliefs that offered guidelines for moral conduct. When the Jodo-Shinshu religion was transmitted to North America, this moral dimension remained effective as long as its members were culturally Japanese, like the first generation (the Issei); but it is far less effective among the younger members and new converts.

What is then called for, is moral guidance that is rooted in Jodo-Shinshu teachings in the new cultural environment. Plus, there must be an ongoing adaptation and engagement with the rapidly changing problems and difficult ethical decisions brought on by new technological advancement (e.g., organ transplant) and social diversity (e.g., racial tensions) (see Chapt. 12).

Jodo-Shinshu teaching seems hard to grasp even for those seeking spiritual answers. Why is that?

That is partly because the heart of Jodo-Shinshu teaching makes sense most easily for those who have tried to climb the mountain on their own power or reflected deeply on the meaning of their existence because of pain and hardships in their lives.

All Buddhists start at the foot of the mountain. Most Buddhists, before Shinran Shonin's time, tried to climb to the top on their own power. Their approach is referred to as the "Path of the Sages based on Self-Power." The formal Jodo-Shinshu teaching begins with the discovery of the existence of a ski lift that was at the foot of the mountain all along! The ski lift is a lifesaver for these climbers who cannot make the climb on their own on account of their limited spiritual capacity. Jodo-Shinshu calls the ski lift the compassionate "Vow Power of Amida Buddha" (see Chapt. 9 on Amida).

The Jodo-Shinshu teachings seem hard because many do not see the ski lift. A few are either too busy climbing the mountain on their own power or just staring at the top without taking a step. Even more are looking away from the mountain at the valley below thinking only about the goings-on of daily life. Still others actually see the ski lift, and ask, "Why should I need that?"

How can we compare the ski lift with the ocean metaphor?

The ski lift is the ocean. It's the ocean that became the supportive and caring reality when the sailor let go.

What can Jodo-shinshu Buddhists do for these people who have no particular need to ascend to the summit and therefore see no need for the ski lift?

Jodo-Shinshu Buddhists must wait until their religious condition matures. We cannot force this maturity upon them. They must come to see the need on their own. But this does not mean we do nothing. We can share our joys of living the Jodo-Shinshu life. Hopefully our enthusiasm will help them reach religious maturity, and they will begin to climb the mountain by their own free will.

Ocean

PART THREE

Spirituality

Ocean

Chapter Seven

Spirituality: Shinjin Awareness

What is Shinjin awareness?

Shinjin awareness refers to a profound spiritual transformation in this life, not after we die. In that experience we find resolution to our spiritual quest. It is generally thought that Shinran Shonin underwent this transformation at the age of 29 upon meeting his teacher, Honen. I believe that his awareness continued to evolve and deepen throughout his life. So, we can say that Shinjin is a kind of awareness.

Awareness is really an important part of Shinjin, isn't it?

Yes. Shinran Shonin referred to it as the "Shinjin of *wisdom*." Jodo-Shinshu spirituality is not simply devotional; it involves understanding, insight and awareness. Failure to understand Shinjin leads some modern scholars to view Jodo-Shinshu as a simply devotional, popular form of Buddhism.

The word "devotion" insinuates that there is no spiritual *transformation* to be realized in this life and that a devotee simply prays for happiness in the afterlife. This view is contrary to what Shinran Shonin advocated. In breaking with the earlier Pure Land teachers, he stressed the here-and-now (see page 57) and transformation in the present life. This emphasis on the present life, rather than the afterlife, has contributed to Shinran's popularity among spiritual seekers in modern times.

By "transformation," do you mean Shinjin awareness?

Yes. Shinran Shonin captures the meaning of transformation when he describes Shinjin awareness as *e-shin*, which means "the transformed mind."

How does Shinjin awareness relate to the well-known Buddhist doctrine, Buddha nature?

According to Shinran the two refer to the same reality, as he states, "This Shinjin is none other than Buddha-nature."[60] Many contemporary Buddhists associate the doctrine of Buddha nature only with the Zen school; they further see it as residing "within" in contrast to Amida which resides "without." This view is incorrect, for Buddha nature and its related teachings such as the Buddha-womb (*tathagata-garbha* in Sanskrit) is talked

---

60 *Notes on 'Essentials of Faith Alone.'* (Kyoto: Hongwanji International Center, 1979), p. 42.

about by virtually all Mahayana schools, including the Pure Land tradition. To compare Buddha nature with Amida Buddha is like comparing apples and oranges. It is more correct to compare Buddha nature with Shinjin awareness. Both doctrines refer to the inner dimension. However, Shinjin and Buddha nature are not possible without the "outer" reality of Amida or Dharmakaya that embraces all beings. Shinran Shonin explains, "This Tathagata (Buddha) pervades the countless worlds; it fills the hearts and minds of the ocean of all beings."[61]

In Buddhism there are many levels of understanding, with the highest level being the Buddha's. At which level is Shinjin awareness?

Shinran Shonin viewed Shinjin awareness as a realization equal to that of the Stream-enterer of the Theravadins, or the Stage of Joy of the Hua-yen or Kegon school. These two stages are accepted by virtually all schools of Buddhism and are essentially of the same level. This level is the initial level of enlightenment at which we are assured of the complete enlightenment that all Buddhas realize. In other words, we can no longer fall back to the lower spiritual levels. That is why it is referred to as the Stage of Nonretrogression. Persons who realize this stage share two qualities: 1) insight into the truth that all

---

61 *Ibid.*, p. 42. The inextricable relationship between the ultimate reality (Dharmakaya, Amida, etc.) and the inner realization (Shinjin and Buddha nature or womb) are discussed in Indian Mahayana texts, such as the *Ratnagotravibhaga.* Inner realization is dependent on the ultimate reality.

existences are not discrete and separate but are interdependent, and 2) absence of doubt regarding the teaching.[62]

Is this level the same as satori in Zen Buddhism?

Satori is a well-known term even among many English speakers. It means many things. It can mean anything from realizing the wisdom of a fully-awakened Buddha, to the gaining of sudden insight about human nature. Shinjin awareness and the insights of the Stream-enterer or at the Stage of Joy are somewhere in the "middle" of satori's range of meaning. Those of Shinjin awareness and other similar attainments have not yet fully overcome greed, hatred, pride and ignorance, which are deeply seated and difficult to eliminate.

If Shinjin awareness involves wisdom, of what do we become aware?

We become aware of the same truth as the other Buddhists. In reaching the first level of enlightenment we are no longer attached to the idea that everything is separate and not interconnected; we become aware of Oneness through our deepened understanding of the Four Marks of Existence. In Jodo-Shinshu, this Oneness is referred to as Other Power or Amida's Primal Vow (see Chapt. 9). What makes Shinjin awareness special is

---

62 The two in Sanskrit are *satkaya-dristi* and *vicikitsa,* and represent the defilements that are overcome at this initial level of enlightenment. This level is also called the Insight Path (*darsana-marga*).

that we also become aware of our own foolish human nature. These two, respectively, are none other than the supportive ocean (Oneness, Amida, etc.) and the drowning swimmer (foolish self) in our metaphor.[63] However, when asked which of the two is more fundamental, I would unequivocably say the ocean. Ocean is the truth which resolves our drowning human predicament!

What other quality does Shinjin awareness contain?

The other prominent quality is the absence of doubt. The elimination of doubt corresponds to the second quality of the initial level of enlightenment common to all Buddhist schools. Shinran Shonin explains:

> Truly we know, then, that this is called Shin-jin because it is untainted by the hindrance of doubt.
>
> (*Teachings* II, p. 228)

The doubt that is eliminated in Shinjin awareness is the doubt we have about the truth of the Primal Vow and its meaning.

> The word hear (= Shinjin awareness) in the passage from the *Larger Sutra* means that sen-

---

63   The two are expressed (though in reverse order) in the famous words of the Chinese master Shan-tao:
"There are two aspects [to deep mind]. One is to entrust deeply and decidedly [to the truth] that you are a foolish being of karmic evil caught in birth and death... The second is to entrust deeply and decidedly [to the truth] that Amida Buddha's Forty-eight Vows grasps sentient beings." (*Teachings* II, p. 213)

tient beings, having heard how the Buddha's Vow arose — its origin and fulfillment — are altogether free of doubt.

(*Teachings* II, p. 257)

In order for us to eliminate doubt, the Vow in this sacred story must come to hold a personal meaning for each of us. For many people in the tradition, the Vow has signified the true caring that exists in the universe and in their lives. The meaning of the Vow must come alive in ways unique to each of us. The Vow cannot simply remain just a story in a scripture but become true and real in the spiritual search of each person. Shinran Shonin expresses this in one of the most often quoted lines in Jodo-Shinshu:

> When I ponder on the compassionate vow of Amida, established through five kalpas (eons) of profound thought, it was for myself Shinran, alone.
>
> (*Tannisho*, p.35)

He is certainly not monopolizing the Vow for himself, but is expressing the joy and gratitude of realizing that he himself is a beneficiary of the compassionate Vow.

I find that to eliminate doubt sounds simple but it is actually extremely difficult. Isn't it also true in your tradition?

Yes, in fact there is a passage in the *Larger Sukhavativyuha Sutra* that addresses the difficulty in a paradoxical and somewhat humorous manner:

> Going [to the Pure Land] is easy,
> but there is no one there!

Shinran interprets this passage to mean that "people of true and real Shinjin are extremely rare."[64] People without doubt are difficult to find.

This difficulty is due to our human attachment, which prevents us from realizing the truth that is already right under our feet. This difficulty is expressed metaphorically by the drowning sailor's struggle to swim, which prevents him from discovering that the ocean is already a caring friend and not an enemy. We need not swim to the distant island. Doctrinally, Amida's Vow contains all the karmic conditions necessary for our enlightenment, and we simply need to entrust ourselves to it.

Doubt is, however, already an indication that the person is seeking and making spiritual progress. A person experiences doubts precisely because he has embarked on the path. Doubt is a natural product of reaching for a higher ideal. You should, therefore, be commended if you have doubt! Moreover, it is the struggling with doubt that enables us to fully appreciate the breakthrough, just as the drowning sailor whose "letting go" was so liberating precisely because he had struggled so intensely.

What happens to a person of Shinjin awareness?

---

64   See *Notes on the Inscriptions on Sacred Scrolls.* Shin Buddhist Translation Series (Kyoto: Hongwanji International Center, 1981), pp. 36-38.

Shinran Shonin spoke of ten spiritual benefits in the present life: the benefit of 1) being protected and sustained by unseen powers, 2) being possessed of supreme virtues, 3) our karmic evil being transformed into good, 4) being protected and cared for by all the Buddhas, 5) being praised by all the Buddhas, 6) being constantly protected by the light of the Buddha's heart, 7) having great joy in our hearts, 8) being aware of Amida's benevolence and of responding in gratitude to his virtues, 9) constantly practicing great compassion and 10) entering the Stage of the Truly Settled (*shojoju*).

Which of the ten is the most important?

The Shinshu tradition has emphasized the tenth, the benefit of entering the Stage of the Truly Settled. This stage is also referred to as the Non-retrogressive State as mentioned earlier. This was a coveted level of realization since the Buddhists were extremely fearful of falling back to lower levels of spirituality. In earlier Pure Land Buddhism, the Stage of the Truly Settled was guaranteed after death upon birth in the Pure Land. Shinran, however, broke with the tradition to argue that this level of the truly settled can be achieved in this life.

For all intents and purposes, when the seeker enters the Stage of Truly Settled, the seeker has realized the highest spiritual goal attainable in the present life. Nothing more needs to be realized, for she has entered the stage that *assures* her complete enlightenment immediately upon her physical death. She is none other than the sailor who, in being allowed to place complete trust in the ocean, experienced the supportive assurance of the immense ocean. In the mountain analogy, this is realized when the tired and desperate climber finds that the ski lift was right under her nose; the lift was there all along, but she did not see or appreciate it. She knows for sure that this ski lift will take her to the top where her spiritual needs will be completely fulfilled.

This assurance is invariably accompanied by a deep and abiding serene joy, the seventh benefit. Shinran Shonin exclaimed:

> My joy grows ever fuller, my gratitude and
> indebtedness ever more compelling!

> (*Teachings* IV, p. 617)

What about the benefit of "constantly practicing great compassion"?

This refers to the ideal in all Buddhist teachings, and of all true religions, of sharing with others the awareness and joy derived from the teachings. This sharing is conducted in various ways: reciting the Nembutsu *Namo Amida Butsu,* making the teachings available to others, supporting the cause of Dharma, and working to enhance the material and emotional welfare of those in need.[65]

---

65   For an in-depth discussion of my argument for a more expanded meaning and role of *jogyo-daihi* than the traditional view that limits this notion simply to the recitation of the Name, see Kenneth K. Tanaka, "Constantly Practicing Great Compassion: Re-evaluation Based on Tokugawa Scholars for a Basis of Shin Involvement in the World." *The Pure Land*, Vols. 10-11 (Dec. 1994): 93-104.

What does the person of Shinjin awareness do?

She does not immediately jump on the lift to climb to the top. She knows she can do that when her present life comes to an end. Instead, she tells others about the ski lift, calling them to discover it. She does not just stay clinging to the lift, for she has a life to lead filled with her friends, family, work and community. And throughout these endeavors, she appreciates the benefits and caring she receives. That sense of gratitude strengthens her willingness to work for the welfare of the community however she can. It's for this reason that Shinran Shonin admonished:

> The person who feels that his or her attain-
> ment of birth (enlightenment) is settled...
> would aspire for peace in the world and the
> spread of the Buddha-Dharma.[66]

I've seen Shinjin awareness translated as "faith." Is that a correct translation?

While some modern teachers prefer to leave Shinjin untranslated, others feel it should be translated into English. The most frequent translations are "faith," "true entrusting," "faith-mind," and "serene faith." In my view, however, no *single* translation will do justice to the meaning of Shinjin awareness. "Faith" is no exception. Shinran Shonin defines *shin* in Shinjin (*jin* = mind):

---

66 *Goshosokushu*, SSZ II, p. 697.

> *Shin* means truth, reality, sincerity, fullness,
> ultimacy, accomplishment, reliance, reverence,
> discernment, distinctness, clarity, faithfulness.
>
> (*Teachings* II, p. 227)

As is evident from the quote, we find some characteristics that are associated with faith, for example, reliance and faithfulness. These meanings, however, do not exhaust the fullness of meaning of this term which contains elements of wisdom (discernment and clarity) as previously discussed.

So, do you think "faith" is misleading and should not be used?

"Faith" is an inadequate translation, as would be the case for any other single word. So, whenever "faith" is used, its limitation must be explained. Otherwise, faith will be misleading.

On the other hand, "faith" does express one important dimension of Shinjin. We should, therefore, adopt "faith" whenever it helps to illuminate the rich meaning of Shinjin. One such area of contribution lies in its distinction from belief. "Faith" is different from "belief." "Belief" in modern language means to agree to a creed or belief only with your mind, without much feeling or commitment. "Faith," on the other hand, means to trust in something because your whole being feels it to be true.

Prof. Wilfred C. Smith, a noted scholar of comparative history of religion, devotes an entire book comparing the two in *Faith and Belief*. He explains the difference:

Faith is deeper, richer, more personal... It is an orientation of the personality, to oneself, to one's neighbor, to the universe; a total response. Belief, on the other hand, is the holding of certain ideas. Some might see it as the intellect's translation (even reduction?) of transcendence into ostensible terms.[67]

This dimension of faith sounds like faith in Christianity.

I feel this common quality does not weaken the Jodo-Shinshu message and shows that there is a universal side of Shinjin awareness that others share. The similarity also gives us a common language that helps religions understand one another. In fact, I was excited to read Professor Smith's further description of faith (not confined to any one religion), for it captures an important element of my understanding of Shinjin awareness:

Faith, then, is a quality of human living. At its best it has taken the form of serenity and courage and loyalty and service: a quiet confidence and joy which enable one to feel at home in the universe, and to find meaning in the world and in one's own life, a meaning that is profound and ultimate, and is stable no matter what may happen to oneself at the level of

67   Wilfred Cantwell Smith. *Faith and Belief* (Princeton, New Jersey: Princeton University Press, 1979), p.12.

132

immediate event. Men and women of this kind of faith face catastrophe and confusion, affluence and sorrow, unperturbed; face opportunity with conviction and drive; and face others with a cheerful charity.[68]

Then isn't there anything unique about Shinjin awareness?

Well, I don't know about being "unique," but as related to the earlier discussion I feel that the awareness of oneself is a prominent feature of Shinjin. This contrasts with what I think is the distinctive feature of Christian faith: awareness of God. And this awareness of God calls for a radical shift in the faithful's will in accordance with the will of God. God clearly plays a more dominant role than does Amida Buddha. God is, after all, the creator. Here, the distinction that I grew up hearing in Buddhist temples regarding the difference does apply, that is, humans cannot become God, while humans can become a Buddha.

Can you give me an example of the idea of awareness of the self in Jodo-Shinshu?

Let me share a poem written by Mr. Goromatsu Maekawa, a ninety-three-year-old contemporary Jodo-Shinshu Buddhist in Japan entitled, Just Right.

---

68   *Ibid.*, p. 12.

You, as you are, you are just right
Your face, body, name, surname,
For you, they are just right.

Whether poor or rich
Your parents, your children, your
  daughter-in-law, your grandchildren
They are, all for you, just right.

Happiness, unhappiness, joy
  and even sorrow
For you, they are just right.

The life that you have walked,
  is neither good nor bad
For you, it is just right.

Whether you go to hell or to the Pure Land
Wherever you go is just right.

Nothing to boast about, nothing
  to feel bad about,
Nothing above, nothing below.
Even the day and month that you die,
Even they are just right.

The Life in which you walk together
  with Amida,
There is no way that it can't be just right.

When you receive your life as just right
Then a deep and profound faith
  begins to open up.

(translated by Taitetsu Unno)

I really like that!

Well, I am not surprised; whenever I share this, many people are also touched by this poem. The message strikes a deep chord within us all. Having said that, however, some may interpret this poem as fatalistic. I don't see that. There is a difference between negative acceptance and positive affirmation. In my view, this poem articulates the latter with a profound sense of gratitude and no regrets.

Now, if you notice, virtually the entire poem refers to oneself and only one line to Amida! This, of course, does not mean that Amida is insignificant for Mr. Maekawa, since all his insights about his life situation would have been impossible without his faith in Amida. Nevertheless, the poem does focus on his newly found awareness about himself and his life. This focus is, indeed, consistent with one of the four qualities of basic Buddhism, personal interpretation (see page 32).

Ocean

Chapter Eight

Ocean and the Drowning Self:
A Personal View

Could you say more about your own understanding of Shinjin awareness? I am interested in something more concrete that I can relate to in a more tangible way.

Let me respond by sharing a personal story that took place a few years ago. I don't want to claim this experience as Shinjin awareness per se. I share this only as an experience that has allowed me to gain a tiny glimpse of what Shinran Shonin must have experienced.

One day as I returned home from work totally exhausted from a demanding day, I slumped down flat on my back on the living room couch. Lying comfortably, almost asleep, I felt a tug on my left sleeve and a murmuring voice calling, "Daddy, Daddy." It was my two-year-old son, Nathan.

I said to myself, "Oh no, it's Nathan. He wants to wrestle with me again. I am in no shape mentally or physically to wrestle with him. Doesn't he see how tired I am? I guess not, and explaining to him won't help." So, I pretended to be asleep.

But my son continued to tug at my sleeve with an undaunted, "Daddy, Daddy!" I became more irritated and began conjuring up all kinds of ill thoughts about my two-year-old, saying to myself, "All he thinks about is himself. Doesn't he understand I'm sleeping? His stubbornness (not to give up bothering me) must come from my wife's side!" But he kept tugging, "Daddy, Daddy." Finally, totally frustrated, I opened my eyes ready to scold him.

Lo and behold...there he stood holding a blanket in his left hand to cover me. He had dragged it from my bedroom all by himself. And his mother and I had not taught him to do this. This was completely on his own!

This scene has been deeply etched in my memory. I still recall with shame and embarrassment, the selfish thoughts *I* had harbored about my son. At the same time, I could not but be amazed by my son's caring act, despite my ego-centered thoughts.

What a touching story! I can tell stories like that from my own life. Do you have other examples?

Well, some college graduates have the false idea that their diploma is due *all* to their efforts; they are like the struggling swimmer who has not yet realized the power of the ocean. But others, with awareness, know that their effort is quite small compared to the support of the institution: taxes, alumni, faculty, staff, tradition, etc. Surely, they made effort, but they are well aware of the support of the others. So, compassion in this example is all of the conditions that allow the student to earn a diploma. These conditions are like the immense ocean that supports the swimmer.

Also, there have been moments when I have felt an acute sense of remorse and guilt about the Vietnam War. Over sixty-thousand Americans of my generation paid the ultimate price, and many still continue to suffer from physical and psychological scars. This guilt extends to the millions of Vietnamese who died and were maimed in the conflict, many at the hands of the ammunition bought by taxes that I paid. Yes, I did whatever I could to oppose the war, yet my efforts are no consolation for the victims. I am not condoning the war, yet I was and continue to be part of the system. I am partly responsible, no matter how insignificant an influence I have in the society.

I am even more ashamed that these remorseful thoughts do not last long. Most of the time I am too busy thinking about my own self-centered pursuits. As the war period slips further into the shadows of our history, I let it slip out of my memory too easily. The fact that I have the gall to even mention this is an example of *my* foolishness and lays bare my shallowness!

What is the Jodo-Shinshu significance of these examples you see in your life?

These examples reveal, in a nutshell, the two aspects that form the core of Jodo-Shinshu teaching: this foolish self being embraced by the expressions of compassion (that is none other than Amida) which embrace me at all times. This truth could not be more revealing than in the example of my son and his blanket!

What is meant by compassion?

Compassion is the caring we receive. This caring includes the example of my son bringing the blanket for me. In the ocean metaphor, compassion is the ocean itself. Doctrinally, the compassion is expressed as the Other Power or Amida's Vow in Jodo-Shinshu.

Yes, the ocean metaphor shows how compassion can be realized when we become less worried about controlling our lives and more interested in letting life speak to us.

That's a beautiful expression — "letting life speak to us"! Yes, as we move the ego aside, the breeze of compassion can blow into our lives. Compassion in Jodo-Shinshu is the supportive ocean. It is there all along, but it does not become apparent until we give up our frantic self-centered struggle.

What other forms of compassion or caring are talked about in Jodo-Shinshu?

We often talk about the love of our family, especially that of our mothers and grandmothers! We also find compassion in the care and sacrifices of our teachers, for example in Shinran Shonin's devotion to his teacher Honen. Many a Jodo-Shinshu sermon has taken up these themes.

I find caring in the things that sustain my life: the sunshine, the rain, the oxygen in the air, and all the beings that are sacrificed for my food. I also find compassion in the beauty and greatness of nature that add quality to my life: the many shapes and textures of trees and flowers that fill my neighborhood, the magnificent Autumn sunsets behind the Golden Gate Bridge, and the Marin hills.

Nowhere is this fulfilling sense of caring felt more intensely than during my three-mile walks to or from work. The beauty of the blooming garden flowers of all shapes and colors enlivens my spirit. At such times I am reminded of a poem by a well-known Myokonin[69] woman named Osono (born 1774):

> *A lily flower*
> *Just nodding,*
> *"Yes, yes."*[70]

These flowers cheer me on during times of personal letdowns. They are joined by the chirping of the birds, whose exquisite singing sound I savor as much as I can. Once a baby squirrel came out onto the sidewalk lured by the rattling of my keys and even perched on my shoes looking for food or its mother. And most of all, the trees are the constant source of my inspiration. The majesty of

---

69   A category of rare, spiritual persons who (since the 18th century) came to be recognized within the Jodo-Shinshu communities for their lives of simplicity and selflessness based on Shinjin awareness. See also Glossary.

70   Ron Hadley, trans., "Myokonin Osono," *The Eastern Buddhist* n.s. Vol. XXVI No. 1 (Spring 1993), p. 1.

their silence is combined with their leaves that reach out by providing the source of life: oxygen. When the soothing California breeze makes the leaves dance, flutter and shimmer in their shades of green, I am reminded of a scene from the Pure Land, "When a gentle breeze wafts through its (Bodhi-tree) branches and leaves, innumerable exquisite Dharma-sounds arise."[71] In such moments, I feel one with Compassion!

I understand the ocean as a metaphor, but isn't this appreciation of nature and your calm due to your own view? Or is the surrounding nature an expression of Amida Buddha? Or are the two the same thing?

Simply put, nature is not a *direct* expression of Amida, but my appreciation of nature stems from my connection (however limited) to Amida. In the language of religious studies, this distinction is referred to as 1) pantheism (nature as direct expression of the sacred) and 2) panentheism (nature along with one's existence are appreciated precisely on account of one's connection to the sacred, rooted in one's personal transformation). Of course, in moments of such wonder and enthrallment, the two perspectives often merge; in such poetic moments, nature and the world do appear (or are experienced) as expressions of Amida!

How is your connection to Amida's caring expressed in its purest and ultimate sense?

---

71   Inagaki. *The Three Pure Land Sutras,* p. 259.

In Jodo-Shinshu this is expressed in the form of a sacred story of Bodhisattva Dharmakara who vowed to liberate all beings once he became a Buddha (see page 70 and Chapt. 9). For Shinran Shonin, this Vow was made precisely for the foolish, ego-centered person such as himself.

I would like to hear more about the Jodo-Shinshu sense of foolishness.

Arriving at the realization that we are indeed foolish is a product of intense self-cultivation to become Buddhas. Shinran Shonin is our model, for he did not see himself as foolish during his early training as a monk. But twenty years of intense training bore no satisfying results. Shinran Shonin found that his greed, hatred and ignorance were deep-seated and truly with no hope of eradication through his own effort.

This discovery, however, was actually liberating. Surely, there was regret and even shame for being so ego-centered, but he experienced freedom in being able to accept his failings: selfish, stubborn, short-tempered, etc.; in modern Jungian psychological terms, he was able to acknowledge and accept part of his shadow. This process is liberating precisely because one has finally awakened to how he really is, stark naked and stripped of all pretensions, defenses and self-images.

Isn't this Shinshu teaching still a little pessimistic?

Some people think so; this is because they understand human imperfection only from an ethical or moral perspective. Sure, some people are more thoughtful, kind, and giving than others. But limitation in Jodo-Shinshu is to be understood in a spiritual context, not simply in the ethical or legal context. The point of reference for our limitations is the Buddha, not the next-door neighbors, coworkers, or fellow students at school.

The more a person comes to appreciate the immense caring they receive from others, the more they come to realize their own limitations. To use an analogy, the brighter the sun shines, darker shadows are projected. The brighter the spiritual light, the greater our sense of human limitations. When a 200 watt light bulb replaces a 25 watt bulb, we see dirt, blotches and the shabbiness of the room that we didn't notice before.

So the realization of our imperfection isn't so much a question of feeling guilt or being forgiven?

There is little sense of oppressive guilt because we simply discover who we really are. There is no one to forgive; Amida is not a judge. There would, however, be guilt if we are trying to be someone we are not. Instead, we become more our true selves.

In Jodo-Shinshu, we are liberated *precisely because* we are foolish, not *in spite* of it.[72] The difference is subtle but profound. For this reason, our tradition does not talk much about Amida forgiving our foolishness but rather illuminating it.

---

72   This expression is from Rev. Tetsuo Unno who spoke at the 1994 Summer Retreat sponsored by the Inst. of Buddhist Studies at the San Luis Obispo Buddhist Temple.

So, if I discover I am an angry person, it is OK to be angry, impatient or violent?

The discovery does not lead a person to feel he has the license to do as he wishes. In fact, Shinran sees such a person being more mindful of not giving in to destructive impulses:

> That he seeks to stop doing wrong as his heart moves him, although earlier he gave thought to such things and committed them as his mind dictated, is surely a sign of his having rejected this world.
>
> (*Letters*, pp. 61-62)

Of course, despite his best efforts he will at times be angry, impatient and even be violent, but not because he felt it was OK to do so.

Is this foolish nature the same as the idea of sin?

Sin carries a wide range of meaning for Christians. If sin means that which one finds lamentable and shameful, then Christian sin and Jodo-Shinshu foolish nature are alike. They are alike in that both get in the way of the seekers' spiritual resolution.

There are, however, differences between the two. Once I asked a Methodist pastor about his understanding of sin. The first example of sin he brought out was that of not taking an interest in the Christian message or Gospel. I was surprised to hear this because it differed so sharply from the voluntary quality of Buddhism. Buddhism regards a person's lack of interest in the Dharma simply as his insufficient karmic maturity but not a serious offense.

145

I realize that my friend's explanation is not shared by all Christians, but, on the other hand, his view is also not a minority position among Christians.[73] I have no intention of judging one position superior to the other. They simply reveal a difference on this point. This distinction reflects two fundamental outlooks: the outward, prophetic Christian orientation versus the inner, contemplative Buddhist reflection.

That is an interesting distinction. Today the word "sin" carries a negative connotation because sin is seen to involve someone else's judgment about us that is forced upon us.

In Jodo-Shinshu the realization of our foolish and incomplete nature is an integral part of our awakening. It is derived from within and so cannot be forced on us because someone else says that we are limited, evil or imperfect. When we awaken to the all embracing caring we just naturally understand our limitations. As in the case of the swimmer, once he saw how immense and supportive the ocean was, he realized the limitations of his own powers. His limitation is, thus, in contrast to the ocean, not in comparison with other people.

---

73   The noted Protestant theologian Paul Tillich writes on St. Augustine's view of sin, "Augustine shows clearly the religious character of sin. Sin for him is not moral failure; it is not even disobedience. Disobedience is a consequence, not the cause of sin. The cause is turning away from God. ... Sin is primarily and basically the power of turning away from God." See his *A History of Christian Thought* (New York: Simon and Schuster, Inc., 1967), pp. 126-127.

I feel that the original meaning or intent of the teaching of sin in Christianity was similar and not judgmental. Unfortunately, sin has been changed in its ordinary secular usage; modern people do not have a good impression of its true meaning.

Ocean

Chapter Nine

Amida Buddha: A Buddhist "God"?

What does the statue in the middle of the shrine represent?

That image is Amida Buddha, described in the *Larger Sutra*'s sacred story mentioned earlier (see page 69).

Amida Buddha is, then, not Shakyamuni Buddha, the so-called historical Buddha?

That's right. It would be more accurate to understand Amida Buddha as an expression of Oneness. In our ocean metaphor, Amida is the ocean itself. And it is the historical (or Shakyamuni) Buddha who appeared in the world to tell us about Amida Buddha.[74]

---

74 This view is called *shusse-hongai* (Shakymuni Buddha appeared in the world solely to teach us about Amida). Others have criticized this as a self-serving sectarian doctrine. Such views, I

149

What do you mean by Amida being an "expression"?

Well, do you recall that Oneness is formless and is beyond human understanding? Shinran Shonin explains that the Oneness, out of deep compassion, took form as Bodhisattva Dharmakara, who eventually became Amida Buddha to establish the Pure Land, and to lead beings to Buddhahood.

> Dharmakaya-as-suchness (Oneness) has neither color nor form; thus, the mind cannot grasp it nor words describe it. From this One-ness was manifested form, called dharmakaya-as-compassion. Taking this form, the Buddha claimed his name as Bhikshu (Monk) Dharmakara and established the forty-eight great Vows that surpass conceptual understanding.
>
> (*Notes on the 'Essentials of Faith Alone,'* p. 43.)

How can we understand this sacred story? Did this really happen in the distant past as the story claims?

I cannot say for sure whether or not this actually took place. But based on what we now know about the history of the universe and human experience, it probably did not really happen. If Monk Dharmakara lived innumer-

---

believe, are found in virtually all traditions, for it is the nature of religious traditions to praise the very teaching that liberated them. Today in our pluralistic society, we must temper such views with genuine respect and opennness for the other traditions.

able eons ago, he would be older than the earth, which is said to be between five and ten billion years old.

There are fewer and fewer Jodo-Shinshu Buddhists who take the story as fact. Especially in North America, most teachers and lay members understand it as a myth. Myth, however, does not mean false or untrue. Myth helps explain a deeper meaning that cannot be better explained any other way. Our appreciation of the myth agrees with that of Prof. Joseph Campbell who so eloquently helped to educate the modern public about the truth and power of myths. There are, however, many people who still see myth as false; that is why I am referring to the Jodo-Shinshu myth as "sacred story" to avoid any confusion.

What is this profound meaning you talk about?

Each of us is part of a cosmic, interdependent network of caring forces, seen and unseen, that protect and support us physically, socially, and spiritually. The sacred story of Bodhisattva Dharmakara symbolizes these compassionate, caring forces.

Interdependence was one of the Four Marks of Existence discussed earlier. Is this interdependence related to the cosmic interdependence symbolized by the sacred story?

Yes. We can think of this cosmic interdependence as representing a *deeper* awareness about the principle of interdependence, one of the Four Marks of Existence. In our appreciation of the sacred story, I become more confident that a caring reality lies just beneath this "bumpy" daily existence.

Many people in the West think that Buddhism only teaches that life is bumpy, illusory, or unreliable. This is obviously a very limited understanding. The world appears illusory only when we remain ego-centered. When we become less ego-centered, we increasingly awaken to the caring world of interdependency. The Mahayana Buddhist sutras are filled with descriptions of the enlightened, Nirvanic reality.

Nagarjuna was a great Mahayana religious thinker, but he talks a lot about "emptiness."

Nagarjuna actually addressed many issues but he has traditionally been known to have focused on the bumpy, unreliable, illusory or empty nature of ego-centered life. Nagarjuna and his disciples of the Madhyamika school made great contributions. They, however, did not say much about the other dimension: enlightened cosmic reality. This side is not ignored and is, in fact, one of the main themes in such important Mahayana sutras such as the *Lotus, Nirvana,* and *Avatamsaka* (*Hua-yen* or *Kegon*). We need to acknowledge the message of these sutras, and not think that Nagarjuna represents all of Mahayana. In fact, the other major Mahayana philosophical school called the Yogacara or the Consciousness-only balanced the scale with their doctrine of Dharmakaya or Oneness to express the enlightened reality. Dharmakaya has since been accepted by virtually all Mahayana schools.

How does the Pure Land tradition fit in?

Focusing just on the question of this cosmic enlightened reality, I see the Pure Land tradition as having presented a more concrete, personified expression of the Dharmakaya. Amida Buddha is a personification (expression in human form and qualities) of Dharmakaya!

So, Amida Buddha is not God, correct?

You could say that Amida is "God," but only if you define God as the dynamic activity of understanding (wisdom) and caring (compassion).

But clearly, Amida is not a personal God who is 1) the creator of the universe, 2) a divine, transcendent being, 3) an omniscient (all knowing) being who knows my daily activities, and/or 4) a judge who decides my final destiny.

These differences become even more clear when we leave the level of philosophical analysis to, instead, compare how the faithfuls actually feel and experience Amida (for Jodo-Shinshu Buddhists) and God (for Christians). It seems that many Christians feel a sense of duty and fear toward God. These feelings are noticeably absent in the way the Jodo-Shinshu Buddhists experience Amida.[75]

Amida has nothing to do with the creation of the universe?

That's right. Though knowledge is important, our knowing how the world or universe began — even if it could be known for sure — does not help us attain the main Shinshu goals of true awareness or enlightenment.

---

75   I am indebted to Rev. Gregory Gibbs' article (January 1996 issue of the *Wheel of Dharma*) for reminding me of the subjective dimension when comparing Amida to God.

To be overly concerned about creation reminds us of the famous "Poison Arrow" parable. A man is shot in the chest with an arrow. He stumbles to the ground. People around him panic, and soon a doctor arrives to attend to him. But the man who is now bleeding badly and barely able to talk, asks the doctor all kinds of questions:

> "Was the man who shot me tall or short, skinny or fat, had light or dark complexion? Which clan does he belong to? What kind of feather is used on the arrow? Is the arrow poisoned? If poisoned, what kind of poison?"

All the while, the arrow is stuck in his chest. Rather than getting the arrow out, he continues to ask questions as he lies dying!

The statue representing Amida Buddha is not an idol, then?

That's right. The statue would be an idol if we believed the statue itself possessed magical powers. It does not. Therefore, we do not worship or pray to the statue for personal favors.

The statue can help to evoke deeply religious feelings in us. Amida's peaceful face sends out warmth and comfort. The statue leans slightly forward, and reminds us of the dynamic cosmic caring that is always actively working to embrace and awaken us.

Yes, I appreciate that. I have close Catholic friends who talk about the deep religious feelings they have when they view their statues.

I've been to cathedrals, and I think I know what your Catholic friends are saying. Feelings are an important part of spiritual life. But feelings alone are not enough, especially in the complicated world that we now live in. We also need meaning.

It is vital that we understand the meaning of the symbols if our religious awareness is to develop and mature. For example, the Catholic church could not have been as dynamic without the contributions of the Catholic theologians, such as Augustine and Thomas Aquinas, throughout its history. To use a simple analogy, many people can drive a car without knowing anything about how the car runs. But you need mechanics and engineers when cars break down or when you want to design new models for the changing market.

When I was at another Jodo-Shinshu temple, its shrine had Chinese characters instead of the statue.

That is an example of keeping that balance between feeling and meaning. In the Shinshu shrines, the main object of reverence (*gohonzon*), which depicts Amida Buddha comes in three forms: 1) the Name (*myogo*) *Na-mo A-mi-da Butsu* written in Chinese characters, 2) painting of Amida in human form on a scroll, and 3) the statue of Amida in human form.

According to Rennyo Shonin, the eighth Monshu, the painting is preferred to a statue, and even better than the painting is the Name. Why was this so? Perhaps, it was to remind his followers that Amida is not a divine being, but a symbol of understanding and caring. Otherwise, we may start to worship Amida rather than being liberated through Amida.

What are you saying when you put your hands together and bow before the shrine?

Na-mo A-mi-da-Butsu. It's the Name I mentioned earlier.

Don't you recite the Name often?

Yes, we do. We recite it together several times during the Sunday morning service, and at the beginning and end of almost all temple functions and meals.

Why do you recite it?

Whether we recite it in a group or alone, repeating the Name is a way to show gratitude and joy. The Name is not a magic charm or a mantra or anything like that. Repeating the Name is not even thought of as a practice or good action that helps us reach enlightenment.

What does *Na-mo A-mi-da-Butsu* mean?

Na-mo is originally a Sanskrit word meaning "to take refuge" (*namas*). And *A-mi-da-butsu* means Amida Buddha. So, together it means "I take refuge in Amida Buddha." *Na-mo* refers to I, the seeker, and *A-mi-da-Butsu* to Amida. When the seeker trusts fully and awakens to Amida, the seeker and Amida become one. This Oneness is embodied in the six syllables of *Na-mo A-mi-da-Butsu*. So, this can be translated, "Amida and I are one." In the ocean metaphor, the swimmer experienced this oneness when he completely trusted the ocean.

Why does the Name *Na-mo A-mi-da-Butsu* stand for Amida Buddha on the shrine?

If you recall, Oneness took form as Amida Buddha to express itself within history. But Amida Buddha cannot be directly experienced in the present life.

Amida Buddha, however, can be experienced in the present life in two ways: 1) in its visual form through meditative visualization and 2) in sound as the Name *Na-mo A-mi-da-Butsu* is heard. Visualization practice entails concentration (*samadhi*) which requires specialized training. Monks and nuns in the monasteries needed many years of rigorous training to do this. On the other hand, anyone who can say the Name can benefit from this second method. For this reason, Shinran Shonin focused on the Name and thought of it as Amida Buddha itself. Thus, in the Name, we laypersons, who cannot build the skill of meditative visualization, are able to connect with Amida. This is why the Name is depicted in the shrine and why our tradition has preferred the Name *Na-mo A-mi-da-Butsu* over the other two forms.

But how can you come to appreciate a bunch of syllables as Amida itself?

We need to learn by personal experience. For most people, the Name holds no special meaning at first. The Name takes on a more personal meaning as we grow more aware, learn to appreciate our life more, and learn more of the teachings.

It is like the experience that results in our saying "Mama!" It is also like the name of one's spouse. When a young man is first introduced to his future spouse, her name is just the name of a woman. But as the romance blossoms, he daydreams and her name churns over and

Ocean

over in his mind. After marriage and the many shared experiences over the years, he comes to identify closely with his spouse's name. In times of need or grave illness, it is her name that he calls. In such moments, he is awakened and reminded of how much he depends on her, more than he ever thought or wants to admit.

Now, when he says, "I love you, Joanna," the name "Joanna" is not just a name. The name stands for the love and gratitude he feels for her support, patience, even criticism. All of these things are the nurturing energy in his life. Without the experiences, the name would be simply a set of syllables.

Still, we must not forget the difference between one's spouse and Amida. "Joanna" is limited to a single person, while *Namo Amidabutsu* refers to our total experience and beyond; the Name (which is Amida) is unlimited, unconditional and universal.

I can understand how shared experiences with a spouse build appreciation for the spouse's name. How can one gain appreciation for the Name Amida?

There is no one method that can speak for all Jodo-Shinshu Buddhists. Speaking for myself alone, I get my cues from the meaning of the word "Amida."

What is the meaning of Amida?

The essence of Amida is infinite understanding and caring, as the name indicates. The name "Amida" is a combination of Sanskrit *Amitabha* (boundless light or infinite wisdom or understanding) and *Amitayus* (boundless life or infinite compassion or caring).

What does infinite compassion or caring mean to you in your life?

I experience infinite caring as "everyday compassion." I find it in my daily feelings of awe and gratitude for the life-giving things that produce, nurture, and sustain my life, whether I am aware of it or not: the DNA molecules, the sunshine, the rain, the oxygen in the air I breathe, just to name a few. Of course, there are the thousands and perhaps even millions of lives of plants and animals I have taken and will continue to take to feed my body.

I can't forget to mention the beauty and grandeur of nature that adds beauty to my life. Many times I have been moved to tears by the sheer beauty of the soft breeze rustling the leaves on the trees that grow on the hills behind my home. There are the inspirations I have from hearing a truly beautiful piece of music, or seeing an impressive artistic creation, or being part of an impressive athletic performance, and much more.

Last but not least, the deep bond I have with my family and time-tested friends are painfully precious. The look on my children's faces when they are asleep never fails to make me smile. My smile shows the joy, pride, and gratitude I feel because they are part of my life.

How about infinite wisdom or understanding? What does it mean to you in your daily life?

I experience understanding in my life as insights, realization or awareness. It's this awareness that helps me appreciate the many examples I just gave of the everyday caring in my life. Why is it I can appreciate them, while many others do not? The difference is this awareness.

It's also this awareness (of life as an impermanent and bumpy road) that helps me to understand the "negatives" of life, such as the funeral of a cherished friend who died at a young age. In my anger, sorrow, and eventual acceptance, this awareness guides me to see life "as it really is" not "how I want it." The funeral reminds me to cherish the present and to help in my own way, however small, to ease suffering wherever I can.

Is this awareness something that you generate yourself?

No, No, No. Awareness started from beyond me; awareness was passed down through the insights and knowledge given to me by my grandparents, parents, ministers, teachers, books, and all other legacies of the religious and secular community to which I belong. I was lucky enough to be endowed with the right causes and conditions for me to receive this awareness. I simply drink the water from the river of timeless wisdom.

For this reason, in Jodo-Shinshu, listening to the Dharma (*monpo*) is so vital. Through hearing the sermons, participating in study classes, and reading books, our awareness is broadened, focused, and deepened. In this process, we are encouraged to become even more aware of the everyday compassion all around us.

So, does all this answer my earlier question about how to appreciate the Amida's Name?

I think so. At least, I hope so. The spiritual meaning I gain from all the infinite caring and understanding in my life gives me proof that Amida's Name is true and real. Just as the many shared experiences with one's spouse give meaning to her name, the everyday examples of caring and understanding show the truth of Amida's Name.

But isn't there a difference between a spouse's name and Amida's Name?

Of course. The spouse's name refers to a single person I relate to on a conditional and ego-centered basis. On the other hand, *Namo Amidabutsu* refers to infinite understanding and caring, whose qualities, in relation to me and all beings, are universal, inclusive, and unconditional.

There is another difference. Even though I say the Name, in moments of deep reflection, I know it is Amida that calls me to recite it. Amida is the source and the initiator. Similarly, it is Joanna's patience, commitment, and love that cause me to utter my heartfelt, "I love you, Joanna." In this sense, Joanna is the source of my utterance. Hence, the *Namo Amidabutsu* is Amida's call to us to entrust just as in the ocean metaphor, when the voice of *Namo Amidabutsu* called from deep within the ocean.

Ocean

Chapter Ten

The Pure Land: Its Spiritual Meaning Today

The sacred story spoke about a Pure Land. What is its role in Jodo-Shinshu doctrine?

First of all, what is most important for Jodo-Shinshu Buddhists is to realize Shinjin awareness, which is gained in the present life. A person of Shinjin is not yet fully enlightened or a Buddha in this life, but is *assured* of enlightenment. Upon death, one is born in the Pure Land where one *immediately* becomes enlightened. Hence, birth in the Pure Land is equal to enlightenment, nirvana, or Buddhahood.

Then, as an enlightened being one immediately *returns* to the deluded world to take part in the ongoing activity of Oneness which is directed to leading all beings to enlightenment. Oneness is a moving cycle of compassionate caring like the river water that flows into the ocean and then returns as rain to nourish all living things.

Isn't Pure Land the same as Paradise as we know it in the West?

Physically the two might be described similarly but there are important differences in what is meant by the different teachings. For example, the Pure Land is the realm of enlightenment where the ultimate goal of all Buddhists, to become a Buddha is fulfilled. On the other hand, Paradise is a realm of leisure and eternal bliss. Upon realizing Buddhahood in the Pure Land, Buddhists move back out to liberate others in the deluded world. Those who go to Paradise do not seem to have that aspiration.

How about when comparing Pure Land with heaven in Christianity?

Christians have a wide range of understanding of what heaven means to them. So, I hesitate to make any quick judgment. I can, however, say that in Christianity there is no doctrine of *returning* to the deluded world as in the case of Pure Land.

Is there really a Pure Land?

According to our teachers, yes.[76] Of course, this is a matter of belief since we can only experience the Pure

---

76 The existence of Pure Land derives from the meditative calm (*samadhi*) of the Buddhas and bodhisattvas. According to the *Larger Pure Land Sutra* Shakyamuni Buddha entered *samadhi* before giving the discourse on Amida. The Pure Land is, thus, not a mere concoction of the human mind but rooted in the long and rich Buddhist tradition of *samadhs*. For further discussion see *Pure Land Sutras*, pp. 13-16.

Land after death. The Pure Land, however, is real for people who have been touched by Amida's Name in this life. For example, Shinran Shonin wrote:

> [Master Shan-tao of China] explains that the heart of the person of Shinjin[–awareness] already and always resides in the Buddha Land (= Pure Land). "Resides" means that the heart of the person of Shinjin is always in the Buddha Land.
>
> (*Letters*, p. 27)

I believe the Pure Land and the Name (as experienced as our deep appreciation of *Namo Amida Butsu*) are one and the same. They are the two parts of the dynamic Oneness. Pure Land is the transcendent (yonder) part and the Name is the immanent (here and now) part. So, realizing one (Name) builds confidence in the other (Pure Land).

Is the Pure Land a place or a state?

It's described as a place, but it is really a state.

How is it described as a place?

The *Larger Sutra* has some wonderful descriptions by Shakyamuni Buddha. Let me cite some:

> The Bodhisattva Dharmakara has already attained Buddhahood and is now dwelling in a western Buddha-land, called "Peace and Bliss," a hundred thousand *kotis* (billions) of lands away from here... In that Buddha-land, the earth is composed of seven jewels—namely,

gold, silver, beryl, coral, amber, agate and ruby which have spontaneously appeared. The land is so vast, spreading boundlessly to the farthest extent, that it is impossible to know its limit. All the rays of light from those jewels intermingle and create manifold reflections, producing a dazzling illumination...

In that land there is no hell; neither are there realms of hungry spirits and animals nor other adverse conditions. Neither do the four seasons of spring, summer, autumn and winter exist. It is always moderate and pleasant, never cold or hot... Again, through its branches and leaves, innumerable exquisite Dharma sounds arise, which spread far and wide, pervading all the other Buddha-lands in the ten directions. Those who hear the sounds attain penetrating insight into dharmas and dwell in the Stage of Non-retrogression. Until they attain Buddhahood, their sense of hearing will remain clear and sharp, and they will not suffer from any pain or sickness.[77]

(*Pure Land Sutras*, pp. 253-259)

---

77 In the earlier Pure Land traditions and most Pure Land schools in the rest of Asia today, those born in the Pure Land generally do not attain enlightenment immediately. They undergo further cultivation. The Jodo-Shinshu doctrine of immediate enlightenment (or Pure Land itself = nirvana) upon death is unique especially to Shinran.

But it's hard for me to believe in such a fairy tale-like place!

The form (jeweled land, trees, etc.) is not what is important in Buddhism. What is most important is that in the Pure Land, one attains nirvana or Buddhahood, which frees seekers from the cycle of suffering.

Though this nirvana cannot be captured by one single description, our teachers of the past tried to speak of it in ways that would make sense to the audience. The first teachers were talking to people in India over two thousand years ago. They talked about the Pure Land in ways that appealed to the people in that time and place. So, this is only one among many ways to describe nirvana.

If so, what are some other types of descriptions?

Our Shinran Shonin speaks of the Pure Land as the "Land of Immeasurable Light" or the "Land of All-Knowing Wisdom" or that "it is infinite, like space, vast and boundless." These descriptions are more rational than mythological.

Yes, I feel comfortable with the more rational description.

I am sure that many people would agree with you. We must not, however, feel that the more rational description is truer or better than the mythological.

We tend to look down on myth as primitive and even false; don't we often use the common phrase "a myth or a fact." Myths are not false, but are sometimes the best way to talk about important things in life that we cannot make clear by using other forms of language.

If there is no soul in the Buddhist teaching, what goes to the Pure Land?

Of the four traditional forms of birth (womb, egg, moisture, and spontaneous), birth in the Pure Land was explained by past Pure Land masters as one of spontaneous birth (*upapaduka-ja*). This is another way of saying that birth in the Pure Land is beyond ordinary thought, or lies in the area of mystery. In Jodo-Shinshu, what is most primary is Shinjin awareness that is experienced in this life. A person with that awareness is no longer overly concerned about how one gets to the Pure Land. She is now able to live with the mystery of the "spontaneous birth."

Secondly, the teaching of no-soul (*anatman*, which we have earlier translated as non-ego or interdependence) is certainly one of the main Buddhist principles. This, however, should not be taken as an absolute truth for all situations. The Buddha spoke of no-soul or non-ego for people who are poisoned by attachment to themselves and to their opinion because of their belief in a permanent soul. The no-soul doctrine is, thus, an antidote![78]

The Buddha also warned that the belief in no-soul or non-ego can become another source of attachment and prevent us from realizing enlightenment. Thus, the doctrine of no-soul is like aspirin given to persons suffering from an acute headache, but the same aspirin will not

---

78   For a discussion on the issue of *anatman* doctrine, see Rahula. *What the Buddha Taught,* pp. 51-66.

help, and might even harm, people suffering from severe coughing. Or, it is like corrective eye glasses to help people who are nearsighted, but the same glasses on those with 20–20 eyesight will make their vision worse. This does not, however, mean that Buddha encouraged a belief in a soul doctrine. He ultimately rejected any absolute position.

So, the no-soul doctrine does not contradict the idea that "something" does continue on to Pure Land?

That's right. We need to see that both teachings (the no-soul and the birth in the Pure Land) share a common Buddhist objective: reducing ego-centeredness and, thereby, suffering. The two teachings are separate paths to the same goal. Because we cannot walk on two paths at the same time, each of us needs to choose the path that is most suited to us. In the past, the monks and nuns generally selected the no-soul path, while many lay Buddhists chose the Pure Land path. Whichever path we choose, we must walk that path with total commitment and sincerity. When we do, we will all be less ego-centered and more genuinely happy.

But I still want to know what it is that continues on to Pure Land. If I were a Jodo-Shinshu Buddhist, I would want to know.

Based on our scriptures and masters, I can only repeat what I said before. Matters related to the Pure Land are in the realm of the Buddhas; so ordinary human beings cannot fully understand the details. It is one of spontaneous birth. Most people in our tradition in the past were able to live with that answer.

169

They did so due, in part, to their ability to accept "mystery," unlike many of us in the modern period who need to know intellectually. You and I are products of the modern age. In my reading of scriptures and commentaries that go back two thousand years, I am always amazed that I have never seen your particular question asked until we get to the late 19th century. In some sense, we in the modern period have lost the ability to live with the wonder of the unknown. The unknown need not always be tampered with, for there is joy and freedom to be realized in letting go of our need to know the details.

Jodo-Shinshu Buddhists, compared to the earlier Pure Land Buddhists, place much more focus on the experiences of this life and not on the Pure Land. Whereas the earlier Pure Land followers needed the Pure Land as an actual place in order to complete their cultivation, Jodo-Shinshu teaching seeks to realize Shinjin awareness in the present life. The realization of Shinjin awareness, then, assures us full enlightenment immediately upon death. So, we need not undergo training in the Pure Land, which thus plays far less of an important role than in the earlier Pure Land teachings. In Jodo-Shinshu, the Pure Land is none other than nirvana or Oneness. After becoming one with nirvana, we then participate in our efforts to work to enlighten other sentient beings.

Thank you for that. But we do live in the modern period, don't we?

Yes, we do. So if we must know, we need to realize that whatever answer we give about the afterlife will be a matter of belief. Belief, in my use of the term, cannot be proven and confirmed by what we can all see, hear, smell, taste or touch.

The one answer that I like is the view put forth by a respected contemporary Jodo-Shinshu teacher, Jitsuen Kakehashi. He speaks of *inochi*, which is best translated "life-flow."[79] This life-flow pervades all things and all beings, including our loved ones and ourselves. This *inochi* is not only a subjective emotion that we feel, but a reality that constitutes the foundation of all existence. The implication that I draw from Rev. Kakehashi's insights is that it is this life-flow that transcends the physical body at death or, in the context of our discussion, that which "goes to the Pure Land."[80] I see this process, however, not so much as "going" but more of "joining," just as the struggling swimmer became one with the immense ocean that all along had existed right beneath him. It is also like a seed connecting its roots with the "ground of being."

What is most important for us to bear in mind is not to fall into the belief that there is nothing after death. The Buddha rejected such extreme opinion as nihilistic or negativistic. Instead, the teaching about the Pure Land

---

79 Jitsugen Kakehashi, "Bukkyo no seimei-kan" (Buddhist Outlook on Life), in *Viaharakatsudo* (Activities in the Area of Vihara Social Work), (Kyoto: Hongwanji Shuppan, 1993), p. 87. His idea is consistent with classical Indian concepts of *bija* (seed), *santana* (stream) and *jiva* (life-force), all of which were attempts to account for "continuity."

80 In the Tibetan *Phowa* practice, a practitioner meditates with the goal of shooting his consciousness up through the top of his head to reach *Dewa-chen* or *Sukhavati* Pure Land.

offers a way for us laypersons to realize oneness with true
reality without feeling hopeless or fearful about the life
after death. In this regard, I am reminded of Keiko
Hirano who died of cancer at the age of 39, leaving a
mentally and physically disabled daughter named
Yukino. Through her long and painful struggle, Mrs.
Hirano found solace in the Jodo-Shinshu teachings. The
young mother left a letter to her daughter soon before
her death:

> Yukino-chan, I'll be waiting for you in the
> Pure Land. When at the end of your precious
> life as you become freed from your body, you
> and I will together become the wind to freely
> run around the fields and mountains. We shall
> also be able to shake the tree branches and sing
> together with the birds. I have a request of you,
> Yukino-chan; when my death arrives, I want
> you to smile tenderly as you have always.[81]

It would behoove all of us to arrive at the same kind
of simple but firm conviction about the life to come. Our
conviction need not take the same form of a wind; our
individual differences will surely lead to other expressions. Some may scoff at her beliefs as fairy tale, but I
would rather have her outlook than that of her critic. I
would rather be a breeze from the Pure Land than to have

---

81   Hirano Keiko. *My Dear Children, Thank You* (Kyoto: Hozokan,
      1990).

no other image than simply becoming ashes or being buried six feet under!

If one does not go to the Pure Land, where does one go?

Such a person will fall into one of two groups. According to the sutras, the first group goes to provisional Pure Lands, such as "Border Land," "Land of Sloth and Torpor," and "Womb Palace." They will all, however, eventually go to the true Pure Land of Amida. These provisional Pure Lands are reserved for those who gain some level of spiritual realization yet still harbor some doubt about the teachings. The second group is comprised of those who have not attained even the realization of the first group. They, therefore, continue to transmigrate in the cycle of births and deaths (*samsara*)[82] until such time as they are transformed by the Dharma. All beings have the potential for liberation through birth in the true Pure Land. Toward this end, Amida's compassionate activities are tirelessly at work to liberate all beings from samsara.

If one is not a Buddhist, where does one go upon death?

The tradition does not give definite answers to this question.

---

82 *Samsara* contains three realms: formless, form and desire. The realm of desire is further divided into six realms or destinies: heavenly beings, humans, *Asuras* (fighting spirits), animals, hungry ghosts, and hellish beings. Pure Lands (including the provisional) are not part of *samsara*, for birth in the Pure Lands represents liberation that culminates in Buddhahood.

And I am not capable of speaking about others. I believe, however, that all sincere and dedicated seekers of whatever religious or spiritual paths will realize the goals set forth by their respective traditions.

I heard from my Jodo-Shinshu friend that at her grandmother's funeral, the priest said she is now in the Pure Land. How would you explain to the family what that means?

I would tell her this: Having become a Buddha, she does not stay there, simply to enjoy eternal peace for herself. She now becomes part of the dynamic Oneness that we can appreciate as the caring force or energy that we experience daily in so many ways.

For many Jodo-Shinshu followers, these caring forces are shown in the many events of their lives: the true concern of friends when we need kind words and a helping hand; the enjoyable and meaningful work that gets us up ready to go every morning; the beauty of the trees cast against a magnificent fall sunset over the distant hills; or the amazement of watching babies whose diapers we once changed grow up into caring, productive adults.

This does not mean that your grandmother literally transforms into your best friend or the tree. It means, instead, that she is part of the unseen embracing Oneness (or Dharma or Life or Truth or Reality) that makes such events and experiences possible at all. So your grandmother is not as far away as you might think.

The Pure Land does not exist out there in the same way that Mars or Jupiter exist somewhere in a specific location in the universe. Instead, it exists on quite a different plane. For Shinran Shonin, while he had faith in the reality which we call the Pure Land, the true nature of the Pure Land could not be fully expressed in words or concepts. This is because the Pure Land is an "existence" that can only be fully appreciated by sharpening our spiritual awareness.

And this awareness can be sharpened by those who take an intuitive and sensitive note of the workings of Amida's everyday compassion in their lives and of their foolish nature. This realization is a little like falling in love with someone. When one is in love, her life and the world hold greater meaning; she feels more optimistic and happy. For those with such an experience, no words are needed nor are words adequate to do full justice. But this is where the similarities end; for such love is limited and insecure because it hinges on feelings of and for a single human being.

For you to fully appreciate the Pure Land and to feel the connection with your grandmother, you must yourself become a serious seeker. If you do not, the caring forces that nourish and support our lives will be shut out from you.

In Buddhism, what our deceased loved ones are doing or where they have gone is of less importance. What is most important is the question of your own enlightenment (*gosho no ichidaiji* – "the most important matter which encompasses yet transcends this life"). Without some answers to the questions of your own life and death, no assurances by the priest will satisfy you. There is a lot of truth to the often repeated statement that when you understand yourself, you'll find true answers about your grandmother.

PART FOUR

Action

Ocean

Chapter Eleven

Karma: Why Do Bad Things
Happen to Good People?

My friend's uncle recently died after a long battle with cancer. He was only forty-one years old and left a wife and three small children. He was a devout Buddhist, a dedicated member of the temple, and a wonderful person liked by everyone who knew him. How can this happen?

Yes, I heard about that. I met him once or twice. He impressed me as a decent and gentle man.

Some Christians would attribute this death to God's will.

Yes, I've encountered that. In Buddhism, we could not say, "It's Buddha's will," because Buddha is not a creator, designer or judge.

Then how do the Buddhists understand this situation?

From my understanding of the Buddhist teachings, there are three categories of cause and effect: 1) objective conditions, 2) personal karma, and 3) Buddha's karma. I do not see that uncle's cancer was due to his personal karma! His illness and death can largely be explained within the category of objective conditions.

In this case, objective conditions point to myriad circumstances that contributed to the illness even though he never smoked in his life. These could include a genetic predisposition to the disease, his exposure in the past to some carcinogenic chemicals, his eating habits, and his stressful life-style. But there are numerous other possible contributions. The specific contributing causes usually can seldom be accurately isolated.

So it was not caused by his personal karma?

I believe so. Some Buddhists may cite his personal karma (the second of the above three kinds of causes and effects). If they do, they have an understanding of karma different from mine.

His personal karmic actions did not cause the disease, because by definition personal karma refers to how each of us experiences or responds to a given situation.[83]

83　Of course within the long history of Buddhism, we find a wide range of interpretations of karma. Prof. Wendy Doniger O'Flaherty recognizes two types of karma: passive and active. The former is "passively received fate" and the latter "actively pursued human action." In her view, the passive interpretation is emphasized in Hindu texts, while the active in Buddhist texts. See her *Karma and Rebirth in Classical Indian Traditions*, p. xxiii.

Personal karma concerns how your friend's uncle responded to the illness and the kind of spiritual insight he was able to gain through the experience, despite the difficulties and pain brought on by the situation.

Does that mean we have no responsibilities since we have no control over our bodies?

Of course not! If you want to enjoy a healthy life, you need to do everything in your power to minimize the risks of harming your body. That means you would refrain from smoking and eating a high fat diet. You should exercise regularly. All of these measures are now openly recommended by the medical profession and many of the government agencies.

But my point is that these actions do not fall within the category of personal karma. They are not religious actions in and of themselves.

Then which category will these actions fall under?

They would fall under the first, objective conditions. All your health conscious actions become part of the complex and unfathomable matrix of conditions that determine your health. Your actions should contribute positively. But there is no guarantee that your action will allow you to live a long life. Look at your friend's uncle. He never smoked, and he led a clean life.

But that shouldn't stop us from taking responsibility within the arena of objective conditions?

Exactly. This is also true in the case of our environment. Most people would agree that the earth is in trouble. There are, however, those who feel we need not worry because it is all part of a grand design and that eventually some supernatural power will fix it and rescue us from catastrophe. This view is troublesome to most Buddhists who do not accept an intervention of such power in the realm of the physical world. If we humans don't do something about the environmental deterioration, who else will?

The same sense of responsibility applies to the social problems of poverty, violence, racism, public health, etc. We are inundated with one problem after another. As responsible citizens of a community, we should do whatever we can. Every positive action will contribute to the overall collective improvement.

Don't these actions have religious implications?

Yes, they can. True Buddhists will be motivated by their desire to actualize *dana* (giving without conditions and expectations) and caring for others in any way they can. So, although the *motivation* may be inspired by one's religion, the actual *results* in these matters are determined by myriad factors that are far beyond the control of any given individual. Such was the case with your friend's uncle.

We are dealing in the area of science and social science. Let's look at the religious arena by turning to personal karma.

Doesn't "karma" mean fate or predestination?

No!

Well, I often hear people say, "I can't change my situation because this is my karma." Or someone

used karma to explain why our mutual friend died in a car accident: "Well, it must've been her karma!"

They are not using karma correctly. First, "karma" means "action." This action takes three forms: 1) intentional thoughts, 2) speech, and 3) bodily action. In other words, karma refers to what a person thinks, says, and does; *primarily in the religious context.*[84] At one level, karma is very optimistic in that it encourages us to realize possibilities that affect the course of our spiritual lives. This clearly differs from the notion of fate.

Second, karma is applied primarily to oneself (first person). It should not be a means to judge others (third person), especially to explain why some people find themselves in unfortunate or disadvantaged conditions. For example, the outcasts, untouchables, and slaves were often told to accept their social status because their situation was their own doing, the result of negative karma created in their past lives.

But isn't karma about cause and effect with regard to what happens to us in our lives?

Yes, but karma has a very special usage. It is the cause and effect in our religious effort to realize enlightenment. Positive cause (= *karma*) leads to a positive result (=

---

84   This is not to imply that there is a religious realm separate from the secular or mundane realm but rather points to the importance of one's motivation and manner in which actions are carried out.
       Karma as a belief system is to be framed within one's attempt to realize spiritual liberation or at least to improve oneself ethically.

phala). Negative cause (*karma*) leads to negative result (*phala*).

So karma is the same as the cause?

Yes. Positive karma leads to positive results.

What constitutes positive karma? How about negative karma?

Positive karma is any thought and its subsequent speech (verbalization) and bodily action that are in accord with the Buddhist teachings leading to enlightenment. For example, being aware of the Four Marks of Existence that I've expressed as: life is a bumpy road, life is impermanent, life is interdependent, and life is fundamentally good. Another set of positive karma is to observe the Eight-fold Noble Path, or to fulfill the Six Perfections (see page 202). Negative karma, on the other hand, goes against or ignores the Four Marks, Eightfold Path and the Six Perfections. Of course, these actions are carried out in the arena of our everyday lives.

What is a positive result?

A positive result is being closer to enlightenment. This means to experience in one's life a greater sense of joy, serenity, gratitude and concern for other beings.

Can you cite an example to clarify some of the points?

Perhaps the famous story of Kisagotami and the mustard seed will help. In that story, a young mother loses her infant child due to illness. In grief and agony she carries the dead child in her arms to see Shakyamuni Buddha with hopes he may be able to bring the child back to life. In response to the grief-stricken mother's pleas, the Buddha instructs her to go around town and collect a handful of mustard seeds from a household that has not experienced a death in the family. The young mother does what she is told with great anticipation that the mustard seeds will bring her child back to life. She knocks on the doors of numerous households without any success, for all of them have experienced the loss of a loved one. With fading hope, she continues to visit the remaining houses, only to encounter the same results.

Suddenly she awakens to the truth that death is universal and she is not the only victim. She realizes that impermanence, manifest as illness, old age and death, is the fact of life. Thus, she is able to see life as it really is and not as she wanted to see it from her "self-centered" perspective. With this awareness, she realizes the Buddha has guided her to find the truth through her own experience. Grateful and inspired to seek full enlightenment, she joins the order of nuns as one of Buddha's disciples.

I, too, have heard this story many times, but where is the message of karma in this?

She created positive karma by following the Buddha's instructions, and through that process, gained insight into the truth of impermanence. Her thoughts and actions were in accord with the teachings. Consequently, she came to experience the death of her child with a more enlightened mind of acceptance, understanding and equanimity. Had she, on the other hand, created negative karma by thinking and acting contrary to the truth of impermanence, extreme unhappiness would have resulted from her inability to understand and accept the child's death.

We can't blame the child's karma for the child's death, can we?

That's right. Just as it was with your friend's uncle, the cause of death is due not to the infant's karma, but to the "objective conditions" mentioned before. So we should not be saying, "The child died so young in his life because he must've committed a grave karmic action in his past life."

Is this mistaken view of karma something like the idea of *bachi* (punishment)?

Yes. The concept of *bachi* is punitive, fault-finding, and backward-looking. It instills fear and does not encourage spiritual growth.

Don't positive results include being wealthy, healthy or famous?

No. Positive karma is not defined by any of these worldly benefits. It may, however, *indirectly* foster them by helping to create a conducive condition to realize them. For example, going to the temple to listen to the Dharma could help a person to find greater peace of mind. He is, thereby, better able to focus on his work or to gain the trust of his business associates because he strives to treat people with kindness and equality. Through spiritual cultivation, one fosters positive "energy" that engenders not only vitality in himself but also confidence and attraction of others toward him.

But once again, these are merely possible indirect outcomes or unexpected windfalls. Positive karma fosters spiritual happiness but does not guarantee wealth, health or fame.

If the results of positive karma are not wealth, health or fame, how are such results to be understood?

The original intent of positive karma was one of psychological and spiritual well-being. For example, the famous doctrine of Dependent Co-arising (see page 22) originally dealt with the process of overcoming existential suffering. This doctrine provided a logical explanation of how ignorance and blind passions lead ultimately to unhappiness, and how the elimination of that ignorance leads to the elimination of the unhappiness.

This teaching, however, was later modified to explain the process of transmigration from past to present and future rebirths in the various realms of existence, for example, as heavenly beings, humans, titans, animals, hungry ghosts and hellish beings. But these interpretations reflect a later development and should be seen as provisional teachings for encouraging people to turn to the Dharma. The Buddhist teachers and writers, thus, adjusted their explanations to the dreams and fears of the general populace. In my view, they had to compromise the meaning to some extent.

What about this third category, Buddha's karma?

This type of cause and effect becomes extremely important in the Mahayana teaching, and particularly in the Pure Land teaching of Jodo-Shinshu. According to Shinran Shonin, as foolish ego-centered beings, we are not able to thoroughly and completely practice positive personal karma. This insight about his spiritual limitations was realized in great measure through Shinran's twenty years of struggle as a Buddhist monk.

In desperation, he left the monastery to seek the guidance of his teacher Honen, who helped him to awaken to the Buddha's karma, expressed in Jodo-Shinshu as "the karmic power of the great vow" (*daigan goriki*) of Amida Buddha.[85]

I sometimes become depressed when I hear about our karma being evil and hopeless.

Well, I understand your concern, but please try to put all this in perspective. Let me use an analogy. Suppose someone you know is a pretty good little league baseball player, and he was even selected to his district all-star team. So among his friends, he is quite good. But let's suppose he was asked to play with a major league team. Wouldn't he feel unquestionably inadequate as a player?

---

85 Westerners who know Buddhism (usually Theravada) for its "ethical," "empirical," and "psychological" features are confused and even dismayed by references to "metaphysical" realities which, in fact, make up vital parts of the central teachings in the Mahayana schools. Further, since the Theravada position is that karma is overcome or cancelled when Buddhahood is realized, the doctrine of "Buddha's karma" constitutes a contradiction. However, in Pure Land and Mahayana teachings "karma" associated with the Buddhas is to be understood as "karma" of a different order, for the Buddhas' activities emanate solely out of a spontaneous, selfless wish to liberate others.

Well, Shinran Shonin was in a similar situation. He was an outstanding monk among his peers, but he had a much higher standard. He wanted to become a fully enlightened person, a Buddha. To become a Buddha through his own power, he had to live up to expectations that were for him impossible to realize, like a little leaguer playing in the majors. He could, for example, not harbor even a trace of pride or hateful thoughts. Shinran Shonin wasn't ethically evil or incompetent when compared with his peers, but he was when compared to the Buddhas. It is only in this context that Jodo-Shinshu teaching illuminates our motives and actions as ego-centric and evil.

How does the karmic power of Amida Buddha relate to my "evil" personal karma?

There are many ways the Jodo-Shinshu teaching attempts to explain a subject that cannot be conveyed adequately through words. We must each experience this ourselves.

Having said that, however, let me cite some examples. Master Nagarjuna, the first of our Seven Masters, uses an analogy of two paths to enlightenment: walking on land and taking a ship. Traveling on foot is arduous and difficult, just as Shinran Shonin found his personal karma to be. But taking a large ship is much quicker, relaxing and easy on the body. Such is the outcome when one person abandons reliance on one's personal karma to avail oneself of the ship of Buddha's karmic power. This is akin to a locomotive switching from a dead-end track to the Buddha's track, which is connected to the ultimate destination.

In our ocean metaphor, the sailor was awakened to the futility of struggling in the middle of an ocean. Instead, he let go of his frantic efforts to keep afloat and lay facing up and completely relaxed. To his pleasant surprise, he found himself buoyed and supported by the ocean. The ocean that was once the enemy became transformed into a supporting friend. Here, the sailor switched from a futile personal karma to the magnanimous power of the immense ocean (Buddha's karma).

Isn't this related to the teaching of Other Power?

Exactly. This idea is central to the Jodo-Shinshu teaching and is expressed in our most important scripture, the *Larger Sutra*. Its main message is expressed in the sacred story of the Bodhisattva Dharmakara. While the story is expressed in a mythic mode, it speaks to the existence of spiritual help beyond the self so long as the seekers' ears and minds are opened to this endowed karmic power of the Buddha.

How does Buddha's karma versus personal karma relate to the idea that we all have Buddha nature? And how does Other Power relate to Oneness?

Let me answer the second question first. Other Power is another word for expressing Amida's compassionate activity. And Amida is the expressed form of the formless Oneness (see pages 27, 150)

The first question is more complex. But to put it simply, Buddha's karma is related to Buddha nature.

Buddha's karma is expressed "externally" while Buddha nature "internally." But in the eyes of the enlightened beings, these are merely provisional distinctions and ultimately refer to the same reality.

How does this all relate to my initial question concerning my friend's uncle?

We become more at peace with ourselves because fundamentally we are embraced and not forsaken by the cosmic compassion. It nurtures in us the outlook that, despite the ups and downs of life, our existence is valuable and meaningful precisely because we are embraced in the universal compassion. This awakening is immensely more important than the number of years we remain in our physical existence, which is ultimately so fleeting. Rennyo Shonin captured this sentiment in the pastoral letter "White Ashes," which is commonly recited at Shinshu funerals:

> When we deeply consider the transiency of this world, [we realize that] what is altogether fleeting is our own span of life; it is like an illusion from beginning to end... A lifetime passes quickly. Can anyone now live to be a hundred? Will I die first, or will my neighbor? Will it be today or tomorrow? We do not know... Hence we may have radiant faces in the morning, but in the evening be no more than white [ashes].[86]

Rennyo Shonin's letter is a rather somber, but true, assessment with an urgent call for all of us to realize the answer to the most important question of our lives, that is that we are not forsaken by Amida's karma to embrace and liberate us.

But this does not help the uncle who's dead.

We really cannot speak for others. He may very well have had his spiritual life in order, even though his physical life was shorter than most.

You must first concentrate on your own existential question: Have you resolved your own religious questions? Your friend's uncle's life and death, a natural part of life, has become a spiritual guide to cause you to think more deeply about your life and its meaning.

Yes, it's awful what happened to him and to the family who is left behind. This must begin a difficult period of adjusting to his absence. Whatever people can do for the family is always in keeping with the Buddhist ideals. We must not forget the truth of interdependence!

Is the Buddha's karma most reliable and true among the three kinds of cause and effect?

Yes. The objective conditions only describe how things are, while personal karma falls far short of the goal of full enlightenment. The Buddha's karma, on the other hand, offers true happiness, expressed by Shinran Shonin:

---

86   Minor Rogers and Anne Rogers. *Rennyo: The Second Founder of Shin Buddhism* (Berkeley: Asian Humanities Press, 1991), p. 255. I have replaced "bones" with "ashes" in keeping with the common traditional rendering.

How joyous I am, my heart and mind being
rooted in the Buddha-ground of the universal
Vow, and my thoughts and feelings flowing
within the dharma-ocean... My joy grows ever
fuller, my gratitude and indebtedness ever
more compelling.

(*Teachings* IV. p. 617)

With this kind of profound and absolute happiness,
"bad things that happen to good people" become the
lotus of awakening in the light of Buddha's caring karma,
growing from the mud of pain and confusion.

**We covered a lot of ground. I wonder if you could
summarize the main points about karma?**

1. Karma is to be applied to oneself and not used for
   judging others;
2. Karma does not mean fate, retribution, predestination or *bachi* (punishment);
3. Karma means action and refers to my thought,
   speech and physical activity. Karma has much more
   to do with the present and the future than the past;
4. When one thinks, speaks, and acts according to the
   Dharma, he or she is generating positive karma.
   Anti-Dharma equals negative karma;
5. Karma does not refer to all cause and effect relationships that affect our lives. Karma is one of three
   kinds of cause and effect relationships, which are:
   1) objective conditions, 2) [personal] karma and 3)
   Amida's karma. Karma applies primarily in a religious context;

6. Karma does not cause our objective conditions. Karma, however, determines how we experience them. The objective conditions are not absolute but are relative. Such conditions can be experienced as good or bad depending on our karmic attitude;

7. Amida's karma is available to those who come to realize the futility of perfecting one's personal karma through his or her own effort;

8. Amida's karma is none other than Amida's compasion or Vow-power. Thus, the Jodo-Shinshu teaching is focused on the third of the three kinds of causal relationships.

Chapter Twelve

Conduct:
Daily Activities and Participation in the World

What is the basis for conduct in Jodo-Shinshu?

While we do not have detailed dos and don'ts, the *Daily Aspiration of Jodo-Shinshu* provides us with a broad framework for daily conduct:

> I affirm my faith in Amida's Infinite Wisdom and Compassion. Reciting his Sacred Name, I shall live with strength and joy.
>
> I shall look up to Amida's Guiding Light. As I reflect upon my imperfect self, I live with gratitude for His Perfect Compassion which surrounds me at all times.
>
> I shall follow Amida's Teachings. I shall understand the Right Path and resolve to spread the true Teachings.

I rejoice in Amida's Wisdom and Compassion. I shall respect and help my fellow humans and work for the good of my community.

How is this practiced?

Well, we recite it together at services, and remind ourselves of what it says as we go about our daily lives. There is another saying, the *Golden Chain*, which was composed on American soil and has been especially popular among the younger generation:

I am a link in Amida Buddha's golden chain of love that stretches around the world. I will keep my link bright and strong.

I will try to be kind and gentle to every living thing and protect all who are weaker than myself.

I will try to think pure and beautiful thoughts, try to say pure and beautiful words, and try to do pure and beautiful deeds.

May every link in Amida's golden chain of love be bright and strong, and may we all attain perfect peace.

What is your religious reason for living up to these guidelines?

It is certainly not simply to be a "good" person. The goal of Buddhism is to become "real" by becoming more aware of the true nature of oneself and of one's relationship to the world. If our motivation is only to be good people, we can easily become self-righteous and bitter when things do not go our way. When we are motivated, however, by a desire for awareness, we often become "good" as a natural outcome of that process.

Then are you saying that each person must first concentrate on improving the self?

Yes, because that attitude goes to the original intention of Buddhism. Remember how Shakyamuni Buddha began his search to understand himself, but not to change the world? "The aim of Buddha-Dharma is to know oneself," goes the first line of a famous saying by Master Dogen, the founder of Soto Zen. In our Shinshu tradition, we turn to the well-known saying by Master Shantao, one of the seven masters of Jodo-Shinshu: "To realize Shinjin awareness for oneself and then to share it with others" (*jishin kyoninshin*).

What about efforts to contribute to the world in ways other than religious?

Yes, they are important and are encouraged as expressed clearly in the *Daily Aspiration of Jodo-Shinshu* and the *Golden Chain*. But efforts to help and to make the world a better place to live must not be divorced from the quest for spiritual enlightenment for oneself and others. So, our number one priority should be to realize Shinjin awareness for oneself and then to share it with others.

What are some of the ways or practices that help you realize your spiritual aims?

The primary activity is to listen to the Dharma which enables us to realize its transformative effects in the context of our daily life experiences. It is in this context that chanting, meditation, and other "practices" are considered as aides to our listening. A Jodo-Shinshu Buddhist can engage in any of the well-known forms of Buddhist practice, even sitting meditation, so long as he or she does not see those efforts as the direct cause of enlightenment (see page 104). The purpose of any of these efforts is to serve as a mirror to increase our awareness about our imperfections and increase our gratitude to our family and friends, the community, and the world.

I like to call these activities "self-effort," rather than "self-power," an ambiguous word in Jodo-Shinshu. Although Shinran rejected the idea that we can actually liberate ourselves through our own power, he never rejected our efforts to understand the teachings. The two are quite different.

Which kinds of effort do you think are important?

Efforts that we can make at home in our daily lives are extremely important. For this, we need to take advantage of the religious value of our home shrine.

Yes, I was fascinated by the home shrine when I first saw it at my Jodo-Shinshu friend's house. It struck me as giving out a uniquely Buddhist feeling.

The shrine can be the spiritual center of daily life. Sadly, however, the shrine is too often associated with death and the deceased loved ones. This was never more apparent than when high school students at a summer youth program exclaimed "creepy!" Perplexed, I responded "What's creepy? How can you feel that way? You should feel safe and sound to be sleeping in the Buddha hall (*hondo*)!" But to no avail, the students wanted to sleep elsewhere and dragged their sleeping bags to the gymnasium.

This came as quite a shock to me. But as I thought about it, it is true that the home shrines are often cluttered with portraits of our deceased love ones; in some cases, so much so that Amida's representation in the shrine can't even be seen. This practice helps keep the image of Buddhism as a religion for the dead and the afterlife. The correct custom dictates that the portraits of the deceased be placed away from the shrine and not within the shrine itself.

How can this way of thinking be changed?

The shrine must be seen as a symbol of the teachings that is important to the spiritual life here and now.

Flower: Represents three of the Four Marks of Existence. The flower stands for (1) impermanence and change, for even a beautiful, freshly cut flower wilts within a week. This fact leave us with sadness; (2) a bumpy road. Also, the flower is a product of (3) interdependence, for without the sunshine, water, soil and countless other factors interacting with the seed, it would not bloom or find its way to the shrine.

Candle: The lit candle stands for greater awareness and enlightenment, or the ending of darkness rooted in one's ignorance. The light of the candle, thus, stands for the fourth of the Four Marks, "life is fundamentally good."

Main Object of Reverence: The Amida Buddha image does not represent a divine being, but a symbol of the understanding and caring that lets me become more aware and thankful for the many factors that support my life (see page 140,159).

Incense Offering: This act shows we are willing to hear and pursue the Dharma. The Indians first used incense as deodorant. Buddhists gradually expanded it to include a symbolic purification of the mind and heart. So when you offer incense you are making a promise to the Sangha (the Buddhist community) and to yourself, "Yes, I will learn, live, and share the teachings."

Incense offering is also considered an expression of honor and respect to the Buddha. And in the context of a memorial service, the same feelings are expressed to the person(s) to whom the service is dedicated. The incense offering, however, does not create merit for worldly benefits or enhance the spiritual status of the deceased.

Your explanation helps to make the shrine come alive. How can the symbolism of the shrine be integrated into our daily conduct?

I encourage each member of the family to go before the shrine at least once a day (before going to bed at night seems to work well). One can then do *gassho* (putting of our palms together as an expression of gratitude and reverence) and recite the Nembutsu, *Namo Amida Butsu*. Lighting the candle and burning the incense would be better, but not always necessary. Then we pause and reflect on each of the parts in the shrine. Moving clockwise from the flower, to Amida, to the candle, and to the incense burner, we remind ourselves of their significance and apply it to our life experiences.

That is an individual effort, but how about something that all members of the household can do together?

Sutra (sacred scriptures) chanting with the entire household at least once a week (of course, the more often the better) helps to bring everyone closer together emotionally and spiritually. Right before dinner seems to work well. Reciting the *Daily Aspirations of Jodo-Shinshu* or the *Golden Chain* together also helps remind us of our connection to the community to which we belong.

Maintaining the shrine can be a wonderful household activity. Each member, including children, can help with the offering of the fresh flower and other offerings such as one's favorite snacks (e.g., oreo cookies), and with keeping the shrine clean and neat.

What are other things we can do daily?

Eating time is a great time to remind ourselves of the teachings. Before and after meals, we do *gassho* as our humble expression of thanks for our food. We remind ourselves of the sacrifice made by the animals and plants. The taking of their lives for food is not our inherent right as humans, but seen as our selfish act necessary for our survival. So eating is a privilege.

"Namo" in *Namo Amida Butsu* can be understood in this context to mean "I am deeply grateful for"; "Amida Butsu" represents all the plants, animals, fowl, and fish that have been sacrificed for our food. So, when we say the Nembutsu, we are more aware of "oneness" with the world. Without the world, there is no I!

I've found these ideas are well-known. But often they have not sunk in, but remain only as ideas in our head.

201

Because of our human nature to forget, it's vital that these truths be internalized through daily reminders.

How about discussions and sharing of religious matters?

Needless to say, they are vital. But in my experience, many families seldom talk about religious matters. They may talk about what goes on in the temple, but such topics are not necessarily religious. In fact, the topics need not always be religious in the sense of Buddhist doctrine and history. Instead, we can share topics closer to daily life experiences that make us either sad, envious, happy, angry, or hopeful.

Through the sharing of these life experiences, Jodo-Shinshu teachings come alive. For example, when we are angry and sad, the cause is usually our ego, though it's often hard to admit or see it. Yes, the person who is "making" us angry may be a real jerk, but we must still remind ourselves that it's our desire to expect him to be at least normal that causes our anger. Such is our foolish nature! Having understood our assumptions and expectations from this spiritual perspective, we are better able to assess our circumstances by coming closer to the Buddhist ideal of "seeing things as they are."

You speak about "right action," and the Daily Aspiration (see page 195) states, "I shall understand the Right Path." What is meant by "right" here? Can you provide a more concrete set of guidelines as framework for bringing the teachings to my daily life?

Perhaps the well-known Six Perfections, a basic Mahayana Buddhist teaching that is usually mentioned during the Jodo-Shinshu *Ohigan* (spring and autumn equinox) services, can serve as point of reference. Please realize, once again, that in Jodo-Shinshu our motivation for following these guidelines is gratitude, and not a desire to be regarded as morally good.

Also, please know that because these Perfections were the practices primarily of monks and nuns, we as modern laypersons with school, work and family obligations will not be able to fully (in fact, "slightly" is more accurate) live up to the high ideals of the Perfections. Nevertheless, they point us in the right direction and clarify for us the Buddhist ideals and, more importantly, serve as mirrors to see ourselves more clearly. The Six Perfections (*paramitas*) are:

1. Sharing (Sanskrit: *dana*): Being open to other opinions and to give of yourself in time and materials without expecting anything in return.

2. Conduct (*shila*): Being responsible to oneself and to others in one's action. The key here is responsibility; we must be responsible for what we think, say and do. However, the Ten Wholesome Actions (perhaps the most well known precepts for lay persons in Mahayana schools) can assist those seeking a more concrete set of guidelines. The ten are:

I shall refrain from:
1. Taking life
2. Taking what is not given
3. Being involved in sexual misconduct
4. Telling what is not true
5. Slandering others

6. Speaking ill of others
7. Being involved in frivolous talk and gossip
8. Being greedy
9. Being hateful
10. Being attached to unwholesome views.

3. Effort (*viriya*): Making an earnest, sincere effort to cultivate ourselves and resolve conflicts and problems.

4. Patience (*kshanti*): Being patient, so as not to expect immediate solutions.

5. Meditation (*dhyana*): Being mindful or attentive to our motives and capabilities in our thoughts and actions. Trying to be honest with our own thoughts and feelings, to cultivate the mind of equanimity with regard to others, and not to always insist upon one's opinion as correct. This mindfulness can be strengthened by reciting *Namo Amida Butsu* (aloud or silently) whenever possible. For those desiring mental calm, you may avail yourself of the various forms of Buddhist meditations, or try Quiet Sitting (*seiza*) (see page 205).

6. Wisdom (*prajna*): This in Jodo-Shinshu is none other than Shinjin awareness. This awareness encompasses our understanding of the truth of the Four Marks of Existence, which help us to see life much more clearly. The Four Marks function like the car windshield wiper on a rainy day that helps us to see more clearly what lies in front of us.

Of these Six Perfections, wisdom is the most important since it is the brain and heart. Wisdom serves as the source of our motivation (e.g., gratitude), energy (e.g., joy), and understanding (e.g., interdependence) for carrying out the other five perfections. If the source is flawed, so will the effectiveness of our actions be flawed.

So, the five perfections are not a means for attaining wisdom (Shinjin awareness). Is that right?

Exactly. The five perfections are not the instruments but are the expressions of wisdom. The five should not be carried out as a condition or requirement for realizing wisdom. When the five are seen as expressions and not as means, then we are freed from expecting rewards or having to judge our performance.

According to Jodo-Shinshu teaching, Shinjin awareness is none other than the Amida's wisdom mind. We are not capable of producing this mind. This wisdom mind pervades as well as resides within each of us. But many of us remain oblivious or ignorant of it. Shinjin awareness, however, is realized when our karmic conditions mature enabling us to awaken to this wisdom mind.

Can you say a little more about this Quiet Sitting practice?

I have found what I call Quiet Sitting (*seiza*) effective in meeting my need for calm and quiet especially during the course of a busy and hectic schedule. I simply sit in a chair with my back straight (leaning against the back of the chair is acceptable), arms resting on my lap and my eyes closed. I inhale through my nose and then exhale through my mouth until my abdomen caves in as air escapes. I repeat this at a natural pace of my bodily rhythm.

Whenever I breathe out, I repeatedly recite *Namo Amida Butsu* quietly or silently in my mind. After even five minutes of this, I am able to feel restful and a little more mindful. And when I breathe in, I think of the many people (such as my children) and current interests that fulfill and give meaning to my life. My very existence is the result of all that I receive from the outside. They are the "power through others," which is one way of appreciating the meaning of Other Power or Amida's Vow. And when I breathe out repeating the Nembutsu (*Namo Amida Butsu*), I am able to express my appreciation in the most profound way possible. This *seiza* can take place wherever you feel comfortable: outdoor, at the office, in your kitchen, in a bus, or before your home shrine.

What is the role of the temple, if so much stress is placed on religious activities at home?

Not going to the temple would be similar to taking a college course by reading the books at home without going to any of the lectures or asking questions of the professor. Not only will it be hard to keep up the discipline to study, but without the guidance and inspiration of the professor and the exchanges with the classmates, one will be hard pressed to complete the required work. The situation would be even more trying than a correspondence course which incorporates out-of-classroom communication with the instructors.

Religious growth depends greatly on the community of fellow seekers. This is especially true for Jodo-Shinshu Buddhists for whom the community of Fellow Seekers and Fellow Travelers (*ondobo ondogyo*) plays a critical role. And the temple is a vital community. Without the temple, there will be few teachers and fellow travelers. Furthermore, Mahayana Buddhists, with its commitment to be enlightened together with all beings, cannot remain isolated from others. It is within this living context that one can fully appreciate the truth of interdependence.

I've heard that some people, including Buddhists, feel that Buddhists are not supposed to get involved in matters of the world. Is that true?

What do you mean by "matters of the world"?

Well, I can think of charities for the underprivileged and also ethical guidelines for such social and medical issues as abortion, organ transplant, and the environment.

The first category—social welfare (what you call "charities")—has been a large part of the Buddhist tradition from its earliest period. For example, selfless giving (*dana*) is a way of sharing with others who need help without expecting any return or recognition. Bodhisattvas are people of deep understanding and caring whose purpose in life is to help others. All Buddhists, by virtue of their spiritual growth, will automatically try to live the Bodhisattva ideals.

The great Buddhist ruler of India, King Ashoka, from the third century before the Common Era, is a prime example of one who lived according to Buddhist ideals. Throughout his vast empire he set up hospitals and drug dispensaries for the sick. He also made the travelers' task safer and easier by building convenient hostels and tree lined roads. The Buddhists after King Ashoka have looked up to him as a model of social welfare and personal humility. Such people are careful not to let their deeds become a source of self-righteousness and false pride.

One such person in the Jodo-Shinshu tradition is Lady Takeko Kujo (1887–1928), a daughter of Monshu Myonyo Otani who was the 21st Abbot of the Nishi–Honganji Branch. During her short 42 years of life, Takeko Kujo dedicated much of her adult life to giving greater voice to the Buddhist women, for which she is regarded the founder of the Buddhist Women's Association (*fujinkai*). When the 1923 Great Kanto Earthquake devasted the Tokyo area, she marshalled rescue efforts for the victims which led to the building of Asoka Hospital in line with the spirit of the Indian Buddhist King. It is said that Lady Kujo died from physical exhaustion stemming from her social welfare efforts.

Today Christians seem to be more active in charities and social issues than Buddhists are.

Before the nineteenth century, I think the degree of social involvement was about even when comparing the Buddhist activities in Asia with that of Christianity in Europe. The gap in the degree of involvement between the two religions started about one hundred-fifty years ago, especially in the United States, when the eighteenth century ideas of equality and liberty inspired such movements as the Social Gospel among some Christians. However, not all Christians agree. Still, even today, some Christians feel that their religious teachings have little to do with social welfare and issues. Religion, they insist, should stay within the boundaries of spiritual matters.

Another important factor for the gap lies in the degree of government control over religious institutions that effectively limited their social involvement. Christianity freed itself from the oppression of kings a few centuries before the Buddhists. In Japan during the Tokugawa period (1603–1867), for example, the state tightly regulated religious activities. The Buddhist priests were forbidden to talk about their teachings to the followers of other Buddhist schools! Further, all members of the family were forced to belong to the same Buddhist school. Do you recall our earlier discussions of the government's oppressive handling of the Sango-wakuran controversy (see page 87)? The situation did not immediately improve even during the modernizing Meiji period (1867–1912) because the government still dictated many of the practices of Buddhism. For example, the government adopted the policy of encouraging the monks of all Buddhist schools to marry. Their Buddhist brothers and sisters in the other Asian countries did not fare much better in their relationship with the state.

Are you saying that the political system in Asia is the main reason for the attitude of many Buddhists toward matters of the world?

Yes, but not all. The Buddhist emphasis on the mind and self-reflection puts more emphasis on personal growth before helping others. We cannot truly help others if we have not helped ourselves first.

Self-reflection helps many Buddhists realize that charities are often motivated by the donors' desire to "feel good" by being a good person or better than others. The good feeling we get when we give to a charity or a beggar is not necessarily bad, but from the Buddhist view can be a distraction. Motivation often determines the outcome of our action. If we hold some prejudicial attitudes toward someone or some groups of people, yet try to be charitable to them, our actions will not be as effective as if we were free from negative views. Again, the aim in Buddhism is to cultivate oneself in order to awaken to how things are and not just to be a good person. One becomes a good person as a natural outcome of awareness. But one should not make being morally good the primary goal, for that would be another form of ego.

But you are not saying that Buddhists should not get involved, right?

Yes, that's correct. I've just explained some of the reasons for my position. Basically, if we understand the teachings, we will automatically want to get involved. Look at Shinran Shonin and King Ashoka and their accomplishments (see Chapt. 4 and page 207)! I believe this is also true for the great people in the other major religions: Gandhi, Martin Luther King, Jr., Mother Teresa, and Elie Weisel, to name a few.

In Jodo-Shinshu, Shinran Shonin serves as an inspiring example, and the *Daily Aspirations* and the *Golden Chain* give us guidelines in clear modern wording. We must remember that our actions are to be rooted in our spiritual life of "expressing our deepest gratitude for the benevolence" (*ho'on gyo*). This benevolence is normally thought of as that of Amida Buddha, but I feel that the source of our gratitude must expand to include much more, i.e., the other Buddhas, family, teachers, friends, society, sentient beings, physical matters, and the universe.

How would you state the basic values for Jodo-Shinshu conduct in the world?

Professor Sen'e Inagi, a noted Jodo-Shinshu scholar and teacher in Japan, suggests the following five values based on Rennyo Shonin's teachings:[87]

1. Listen to the teachings throughout one's life,
2. Refrain from quarreling with other schools and religions,
3. Fully actualize the mind of equality (*byodo-shin*) that sees and treats people and events in our lives with equanimity,
4. Respect and honor life,
5. Abandon superstitious and magical practices.

Can you possibly offer some more concrete guidelines, particularly with regard to social issues?

I must start by telling you that the following guidelines are the view of one person and are not intended to speak for any group or to be regarded as mandatory for Shinshu Buddhists. They should certainly not be thought of as a practice or means for realizing Shinjin awareness. They are intended, instead, to address a need among many American Shinshu Buddhists for a practical framework to

---

87   Inagi Sen'e. *Jodo-Shinshu no rinri* (Ethics in Jodo-Shinshu) (Kyoto: Tankyusha, 1987), pp. 100–119.

think about today's social issues from their religious perspective.

I have concentrated on four of today's ethical topics: abortion, social welfare, capital punishment, and environment. After each point, "( )" denotes the topic/s among the four that are more impacted and "[ ]" indicates parallel ideas found in statements and preambles in existing Shinshu service books.

1) I believe the world-universe in which we find ourselves, despite its downside and tragedies, is fundamentally compassionate. This vision finds expression in the *Larger Sutra's* Bodhisattva Dharmakara whose selfless sacrifices aspire to spiritually nourish and liberate all sentient beings (all four issues) [*Jodo-Shinshu Preamble* (See Appendix III) and *Daily Aspiration*].

2) The universe is an interconnected network in which I play a vital role. As a member of this community, I must do my share to contribute to its welfare. We cannot wistfully depend on transcendent beings to bail us out from the grave environmental, medical, and social crises that now threaten the survival of the world (social welfare, environment) [*Preamble, Daily Aspirations, Golden Chain, Pledge*].

3) In making my contribution to the world, I should not be motivated by a desire to be a "good person" or feel righteous that I have done a "good deed." What I give back to the world pales in comparison to what I receive from the world. Plus, given my ego-centered ways, a "good" deed today will quickly be snuffed out tomorrow,

or even the next moment, by acts driven by selfish motives. Shinran speaks to this:

> *Difficult is it to be free of evil nature*
> *The heart is like snake and scorpion*
> *Good acts also are mixed with poison*
> *They are but deeds vain and false.*
>
> (social welfare) [*Preamble*]

4) I believe that most criminal offenses are a result of causes and conditions reflecting the socio economic environment of the offender. Though the offender must bear the responsibility for his or her actions, as a member of society I should help correct the underlying social problems as well as help rehabilitate the offender. Furthermore, I should not feel righteous in looking down upon these people, for I am reminded of Shinran's insight:

> It is not that you keep from killing because
> your heart is good. In the same way, a person
> may wish not to harm anyone and yet end up
> killing a hundred or thousand people.
>
> (*Tannisho*, Chapter 13)

5) I believe there are no absolutes in matters of the conventional, everyday world. Crucial issues, in particular, involve complex sets of factors and yield no ready-made, black and white answers (abortion).

6) If at all possible, utmost effort must be made to preserve and foster life, and not to take life (abortion, capital punishment) [first of the Five Precepts, Precepts in the Six Paramitas].

7) If I must terminate life, utmost care should be taken to be well informed about the subject matter. The decision making must include a serious consideration for the welfare of all whose lives would be impacted; for a person is involved in a much wider interconnected set of relationships (abortion, capital punishment, environment).

8) Whatever decision I make, I must be willing to bear my share of the responsibility for its consequences and not shift blame or responsibility onto others (abortion, capital punishment, environment) [*Preamble*].

9) I do not make my ultimate aim in life to accumulate wealth, gain fame or garner power (social welfare, environment) [*Preamble, Aspiration, Golden Chain*].

10) I strive to live simply and to share my energy, time and resources for the betterment of the world (social welfare, environment) [*Preamble, Daily Aspiration, Golden Chain*].

11) I strive to refrain from idle talk and to neither purposely create discord among people nor speak ill of others without any constructive intention. (social welfare) [*Preamble*]

12) I do not feel any need to consult or petition supernatural forces to satisfy worldly objectives or to allay fears and anxieties stemming from such forces. I, therefore, do not rely on horoscope reading, fortune-telling, or superstitious beliefs to serve as a guide in my life. [*Preamble*].

How would you approach matters related to sexuality and gender issues from a Jodo-Shinshu perspective?

I recently was asked to provide an answer to that same question for an article, "Sexual Ethics in Religious Institutions" in a newspaper. The categories were provided, and I responded with the following:

Buddhism is concerned primarily with personal awakening to the spiritual truth of wisdom or understanding and compassion or caring. Because Buddhist spiritual insights do not produce automatic, black-and-white answers concerning ethical matters that apply to all people and all circumstances, individual Buddhists are encouraged to think for themselves in arriving at their own conclusions based upon their spiritual insights. The teachings are not about one's adherence to a rigid moral set of absolute right and wrong. Consequently, Buddhist groups have generally refrained from taking absolutist positions on ethical issues, including most of the sexual-ethical issues being considered in this survey. (Of course, this does not apply to the monks and nuns who take vows to observe strict precepts related to sex.)

Although spiritual insights do not lead to ethical absolutes, there are some basic principles on which an individual may choose to base his or her ethical decisions. They can be expressed as: 1) I shall try to be mindful and take responsibility for my actions, 2) I shall try not to bring pain to others, and 3) I shall try not to be judgmental of others because I, too, am far from being perfect.

The views expressed below are those of one individual and do not speak for the Buddhist Churches of America or any other Buddhists; they are meant for the householders (non-monastic clergy and lay) within the contemporary American context.

Teenage Sex: Strongly discouraged since, due to their immaturity, teenagers generally take neither full responsibility nor precautions for the potential consequences of pregnancy and disease.

Premarital Sex: Strongly discouraged for minors for the same reason as above. Adults, on the other hand, are encouraged to be mindful of the three basic principles (See above).

Masturbation: No basic problem or moral stigma attached to the act.

Extramarital Sex: Strongly discouraged since it brings pain upon the spouse and family and shows a lack of responsibility for one's marital commitment.

Divorce: Not prohibited or condemned if all sincere attempts to work out the differences have been exhausted.

Abortion: Discouraged but does not condemn those who after having exhausted all other options found no recourse but to abort; they then should take responsibility and reflect upon future actions.

Contraception: Accepted.

Married Clergy: Believing that members of the clergy should enter marriage and experience normal life, the founder of the school, Shinran, married after twenty years as a monk and had several children. Most Jodo-Shinshu priests have married throughout the school's 800 year history, making it unique among Buddhist schools, although in recent modern times other Japanese Buddhist schools allow their clergy to marry.

Female Clergy: Accepted. Three out of the sixty priests in the Buddhist Churches of America are female. No doctrinal grounds to prohibit or discourage the ordination of women. Other American BCA women have been ordained.

Homosexual Orientation: Not condemned. No doctrinal grounds exist for a judgmental attitude by others. All beings are equally embraced by Amida Buddha, the symbol of understanding and caring.

Homosexual Acts: Not condemned; keeping of the three principles are encouraged.

Same-Sex Blessings in Churches: Accepted.

Ordination of Homosexuals: Not prohibited. No doctrinal grounds exist for barring candidates for this reason.

How would you sum up the Jodo-Shinshu outlook on conduct and participation in the world?

I cannot help but look to Shinran Shonin, whose life of ninety years was dedicated to reaching out to the world by sharing the teachings in person and through writings. This spirit is exemplified by the fact that virtually all chantings during Jodo-Shinshu services conclude with a verse:

> *May this merit-virtue*
> *Be shared equally with all beings*
> *May we together awaken the Bodhi Mind,*
> *And be born in the realm of Serenity and Joy.*

Ocean

Epilogue

A Life of Naturalness: Another Buddhist Model

In the West the heroic model of Buddhism predominates. This is well exemplified in the life story of Shakyamuni Buddha. In the well-known legendary biography, he forsakes his throne and family, rides off into the forest on a white horse, endures the life of an ascetic for six years, conquers temptations to become the Awakened One, and then roams throughout the region for the next forty-five years with his throng of disciples to spread the Dharma. Other models from East Asia include the "antics" of enlightened masters who shout and beat their disciples to awakening, and admonish "When you meet the Buddha, kill him!" Thus, the heroic model is characterized by the assertive, ascetic, serious, non-familial, individualistic, and extraordinary.

The heroic exemplars do, indeed, attract our attention and even our fervent loyalty. Their attraction stems, in part, from their accomplishments which we know we can only mimic but never fully emulate. There are, however, many who cannot be satisfied with that. They seek a model that they themselves can reach within the everyday and the mundane for ordinary people. They cannot and do not want to forsake the world, their family and work. Surely, there is room for other Buddhist models for North Americans to adopt.

I believe we have witnessed in the previous chapters of this book an emergence of another image, one that is more receptive than assertive, more sensitive than ascetic, more humorous than serious, more family-oriented, more community-centered than individualistic and more ordinary than extraordinary. Perhaps, this alternative model can lend another perspective to helping us to arrive at our personal spiritual resolution. The insights and values of the Jodo-Shinshu model can similarly contribute to the development of a new ethos for relating to the challenges of a world that is becoming increasingly pluralistic and interdependent.

I wish to share a story that illustrates this model.[88] This story was told to us by the late Rev. Chijun Yakumo, who in my estimation represented the best qualities of the approximately one thousand Jodo-Shinshu priests

---

88   This is adapted from a Japanese essay told by the late Rev. Chijun Yakumo.

and their spouses who crossed the Pacific Ocean during the past one hundred years. With a deep sense of appreciation for their dedication and struggles to transmit the Jodo-Shinshu teachings to these North American shores, I shall conclude with that wonderful story from Japan.

Once upon a time in a small village in the southern part of the island of Honshu, there were two Buddhist temples, one of the major monastic schools and the other Jodo-Shinshu. The tiny village of some sixty families could no longer afford to support both temples. The villagers had to choose one and abandon the other. They decided to hold a contest to see which of the two (the monk or the priest) was more fit to be their spiritual leader.

When the day of the contest came, a large group of villagers gathered in the village plaza where they had set up a large vat of boiling water. They asked the two, "What will you do with this?"

The monk stood up first. He was tall and well-built. His frame had been made impressive by the long, hard training required by his school. He stepped up to the vat with confidence and slowly lowered himself into the boiling pot. The head-shaven monk recited the *mantras* (sacred words), performed *mudras* (sacred gestures of the hands and fingers) and focused his mind. It was an impressive sight. The boiling water did not seem to bother the monk at all as he calmly dipped all the way in until his shoulders were completely immersed. The villagers looked on in awe and were extremely impressed by the monk. The monk stepped out of the cauldron in mindfulness without any visible signs of a burn.

Now it was the Jodo-Shinshu priest's turn. He turned to the villagers and asked them to bring some large wooden tubs filled halfway with cold water. The villagers thought it was a strange request, but they did as he asked. As the tubs arrived, the Shinshu priest poured hot water from the vat into the tubs to make them lukewarm. He then said, "This is perfect for a hot-tub dip! But it's a waste for me to enjoy this by myself. Won't you all join me and enjoy this tub?" Many of the villagers did join the Shinshu priest. In time, the villagers began to appreciate the warm water and the camaraderie. Some even began to sing! They had a great time!

The villagers were impressed with the monk's extraordinary abilities, but wondered what would happen after he died. His personal accomplishments and training would be of little use once he was gone. On the other hand, the Jodo-Shinshu priest showed no special abilities. He seemed like one of them, yet he lived by the ideals of sharing, humility, and finding joy in doing ordinary things. This teaching could be practiced by every villager and would live on beyond the priest's lifetime. So the villagers decided in favor of the Jodo-Shinshu priest and his temple!

This story shows how the teachings of the ordinary can be more compelling and lasting than those of the extraordinary. The "ordinary" Shinshu priest remained true to the Buddhist truth of non-attachment to one's ego. By showing his unselfish side, he was teaching the villagers that it is good to share joy together and that we depend on one another.

Lastly, I am reminded of one of my favorite utterances by Shinran Shonin's statement, "Now, whether you accept the Nembutsu, entrusting yourself to it, or reject it, that is your own decision" (*Tannisho,* p. 7). I do hope, however, that you do not reject it and that you seek to deepen your understanding. I invite you to explore the resources listed below. My best wishes to you as we walk the paths together.

Ocean

Appendix I

Key Historical Dates

<u>Buddhist/Jodo-Shinshu</u>	<u>Christianity</u>

600 B.C.E.
    Shakyamuni Buddha born
    (ca. 560)	

500	
400	

300
    King Ashoka takes reign
    (268)
200	

100 Mahayana Buddhism emerges	
0 (C.E.)	Jesus of Nazareth born
200 Nagarjuna (Ryuju)	

300
                                        Christianity becomes religion
                                        of Roman Empire (early 4th c.)

400
    Vasubandhu (Tenjin)   Augustine strengthens
                                          Christian position (354-430)

500
    T'an-luan (Donran)

600
    Tao-ch'o (Doshaku)

700

800
                                          Charles Martel crowned Holy
                                          Roman Emperor (800)

900
    Genshin

1000
                                          Split of the Roman and
                                        Orthodox Churches (1054)

1100
    Shinran born (1173)   First Crusades (1096–99)
    Honen claims independence
    of Pure Land school (1175)

1200
    Shinran dies (1263)   Thomas Aquinas (1225–74)

    Shinran's daughter
    Kakushinni donates property
    (1277)

    Honganji main hall built
    (1338)

1400
> Rennyo rebuilds main
> temple (1482)

1500
> Shogun Nobunaga begins
> 10 year siege of Osaka
> temple (1570)

Martin Luther initiates the
Protestant movement (1517)

1600

Pilgrims arrive in North
America (1620)

1700

1800
> Government settles *Sango
> wakuran* doctrinal contro-
> versy (1806).
>
> Jodo-Shinshu missionaries
> arrive in Hawaii (1889) &
> the mainland (1899)

Social Gospel movement in
U.S. Historical method
challenges Biblical assumptions

1900
> Mainland U.S. branch
> renamed:
> Buddhist Churches of
> America (1944)

Second Vatican Council to
liberalize Catholic ritual and
theology (1962-1965)

Ocean

228

Appendix II

Life Chronology of Shinran Shonin

Year	Age	Event
1173		Born in Hino, outskirts of Kyoto
1181	9	Takes ordination and begins a 20 year period as a novice and later a monk on Mt. Hiei
1201	29	Leaves monastery on Mt. Hiei and becomes Honen's student
1207	35	Exiled to Echigo on the Japan Sea side
1211	39	Pardoned
1212	40	Teacher Honen dies
1214	42	Moves to Kanto (near present day Tokyo) area to work with ordinary class of people
1234	62	Returned to Kyoto (the exact year not conclusive) to devote to writing
1263	90	Dies in Kyoto

Ocean

Appendix III

Kyosho: Preamble of Jodo Shinshu

Name: Jodo-Shinshu Hongwanjiha

Founder: Shinran Shonin (1173–1263)

Central Object of Reverence:
               Amida Tathagata (Namo Amida Butsu)

Sutra: Three Principal Sutras of Jodo Shinshu

    1. *Sutra on the Buddha of Infinite Life*
       (*Daikyo* — Larger Sutra)

    2. *Sutra of Meditation on the Buddha of Infinite Life*
       (*Kangyo* — Contemplation Sutra)

    3. *Sutra on the Amida Buddha*
       (*Shokyo* — Smaller Sutra)

Teaching: Having entrusted ourselves to the teaching
               of Namo Amida Butsu, we experience the
               joy of having received the assurance of
               Buddhahood. From the constant gratitude
               that arises within, we shall strive to live in
               service to the community and humanity.

Tradition: The Honpa Hongwanji* is a community of
               people joined together in the joy of a com-
               mon faith in Amida Buddha. As Jodo Shin-
               shu Buddhists, we shall seek to be mindful
               of our words and deeds, be responsible

231

citizens of our society, and share with
others the truth and reality of Jodo-Shinshu. Understanding fully the principle of
causality, we shall not practice petition and
prayer or magic, nor shall we rely upon
astrology or other superstitions.

[*Shin Buddhist Service Book,*
published by the Buddhist Churches of America, 1994]

*Note: "Hongwanji" is the official English rendering
utilized by the Honpa Hongwanji tradition, and is thus
employed here. This is in contrast to "Honganji" used
elsewhere in this book.

Appendix IV

The Ten Branches of the

Jodo-Shinshu School

The first two branches are today by far the largest and also trace their line through Shinran's blood descendants. Kaku'nyo (its 3rd abbot, 1270–1351) played a crucial role in the creation of the transmission line. The split into the two branches took place around 1580 (see pages 86).

1. Hongwanji-ha (Nishi or West):
   After Kennyo (11th abbot), followed by second son Junnyo.

2. Otani-ha   (Higashi or East):
   After Kennyo, followed his first son Kyo'nyo.

3. Kibe-ha: Founded by those in the Omi Province (present day Shiga Prefecture, east of Kyoto) who were converted by Shinran on his return to Kyoto from Kanto.

4. Izumoji-ha: Founded by Josen, a disciple of Kaku'nyo, in the Tamba area, but later moved to the Echizen area on the Japan Sea side.

5. Bukkoji-ha: Established in 1324 by Ryogen who established a temple in Kyoto. According to

temple history, Shinran established the first temple and his direct disciple Shinbutsu named it Koshoji.

6. Koshoji-ha: Kyogyo, the 14th abbot of the Bukkoji Branch broke away from its branch and established Koshoji Temple in Kyoto. The new temple became affiliated with the Honganji Branch until its independence in 1876.

7. Takada-ha: Founded by Shinran's direct disciple Shinbutsu of Takada in Kanto area (close to Tokyo).

These last three branches were all founded by Nyodo in the 14th century in the Echizen area on the Japan Sea side. Their independent branch status was recognized in 1878.

8. Yamamoto-ha: After Nyodo, it followed the Dosho and Zenju line.

9. Joshoji-ha: After Nyodo, it followed the Dosho and Nyokaku line.

10. Sammonto-ha: After Nyodo, it followed the Nyojo line.

The vast majority of the Jodo-Shinshu Buddhists in North America belong to Honganji-ha Branch as members of one the three *kyodans* (teaching groups): Buddhist Churches of America (mainland), Honpa Honganji Mission of Hawaii and the Buddhist Churches of Canada. They represent approximately 200 temples, fellowships and branches.

The Otani-ha is the only other branch to be represented with approximately six temples in Hawaii and four on the mainland. No other branches are represented in North America. There are two independent Jodo-Shinshu temples (Chicago and Hawaii).

Ocean

Appendix V

Resources in North America:

Jodo-Shinshu Nishi-Honganji Branch Affiliated

Buddhist Churches of America:
>   1710 Octavia St., San Francisco, California 94109
>   Tel. (415) 776-5600; Fax (415) 771-6293

>   Bookstore (Tel. 415-776-7877):
>   Sells books, other instructional materials, ritual
>   items including affordable home shrines. Operates
>   a good mail order system; ask for catalogue.

>   Headquarters: Primarily serves the administrative
>   functions for the approx. 100 temples, fellowships
>   and branches on the continental U.S. Please inquire
>   about the affiliate membership program available
>   especially to those not living near a temple.

Institute of Buddhist Studies: Seminary and Graduate
School:
>   650 Castro St. Suite 120-202
>   Mt. View, CA 94041
>   Tel. (650) 938-7192; Fax (650) 938-5937

>   Offers one degree: Master of Arts in Buddhist
>   Studies (academic degree offered jointly with
>   the Graduate Theological Union). Extra courses
>   are required for the priesthood.

Honpa Hongwanji Mission of Hawaii:
    1727 Pali Highway, Honolulu, HI 96813
    Tel. (808) 522-9200; Fax (808) 522-9209

    Headquarters for the approximately 36 temples
    serving the state of Hawaii.

Buddhist Study Center:
    1436 University Ave., Honolulu, HI 96822
    Tel. (808) 946-9660

    The research and educational center serving both
    the Jodo-Shinshu and larger communities. Locat-
    ed adjacent to Univ. of Hawaii, the Center also
    serves as a campus drop-in center.

Buddhist Churches of Canada:
    4860 Garry St., Richmond,
    British Columbia, Canada V7E 2V2
    Tel. (604) 272-6865; Fax (604) 272-6865

    Headquarters for the approximately 20 temples,
    branches and fellowships serving Canada.

Dohboh Sangha De Mexico AC:
    Eugenia No. 17. Col. Napoles. C.P. 03840,
    Mexico D.F. Mexico
    Tel. 011-52-5-543-0507 (from outside Mexico)
    Fax. 011-52-5-523-2673

Jodo-Shinshu Selected Web-sites

Dr. Alfred Bloom: http://www.aloha.net/~albloom/sdn/

Shin Buddhist Resource Center: http://www.fogbank.com/sbrc/

Ryukoku University, Kyoto:
http://www.ryukoku.ac.jp/English/menu-e.htm

The White Path Temple: http://www.mew.com/shin/

Vista Temple: http://www.geocities.com/~shoken-ji

Appendix VI

When Confronted by Non-Buddhist Fundamentalists

It's often a daunting experience trying to fend off solicitations and sometimes even verbal attacks by strong-willed, uncompromising religious fundamentalists. We experience them on college campuses and on our doorsteps. This section is meant to assist Buddhists, Jodo-Shinshu Buddhists in particular, in dealing effectively with such situations.

Fundamentalists, as I define them here, refer to those who adhere to certain values and worldview. They are not exclusive to any one religious tradition. Instead, fundamentalists are found among all the major world religions, including Buddhism. However, we shall be focusing on the non-Buddhist fundamentalists because they are the ones who pose the greatest challenge to the Buddhists in North America.

First, we must remind ourselves of the Jodo-Shinshu Buddhist attitude toward others:

1. **Respectful:** We respect other religions, and refrain from quarreling with others on differences of belief. "Among the Nembutsu followers of this sect there

must not be slander of any of the other teachings."
(Rennyo Shonin)

2. **Voluntary:** Choice of religion is personal and voluntary. "Now, whether you accept the Nembutsu, entrusting yourself to it, or reject it, that is your own decision." (Shinran Shonin)

3. **Oneness:** All people and beings are interconnected to make up the same order of reality. "All beings have been fathers and mothers, brothers and sisters, in the timeless process of birth-and-death." (Shinran Shonin)

Next, we must be aware of the basic beliefs and values of the fundamentalists in order to know "where they're coming from." They can be generalized as follows:

1. **The Book as absolute:** The entire Book, not just parts, is inspired by God. Therefore, there can be no errors. Everything in the Book is understood as the literal, factual word of God.

2. **Devil or Satan as real:** He and other hosts of demons are believed capable of demonic possessions. They also account for personal tragedies and strange happenings in the world.

3. **Humanity as sinful:** All humans have sinned. Humans fall far short of the glory of God. Sin, if left unattended, results in death.

4. **They as the chosen people:** When the world undergoes tribulations and eventual destruction, only they will be saved. God will remove them and secure their place in the new kingdom of God.

5. **God as wrathful**: While they may emphasize the love of God for evangelical purposes, they are quick to remind people of the wrath and judgment of God for those who reject the teaching.

Ocean

Glossary:

In 25 Words or Less

This glossary is intended to provide the most basic understanding of the key words that appear throughout the book. For the other key words that appear less frequently, please use the Index for locating the discussions in the book itself.

Since the entire book is, in essence, a glossary of sorts, the reader is encouraged to refer to the main section of the book for clarification. For that purpose, the page numbers of *primary* discussions are provided at the end of each definition. For locating *other* discussions of the same word, please utilize the Index.

* = terms that are also found in the Glossary

Amida Buddha: Buddha that symbolizes the compassionate dimension of Oneness,* which is experienced when we become aware of the personal appreciation of the sacred Name* *Namo Amida Butsu**.

Anatman or **Anatta** (**muga** 無我): One of the Four Marks of Existence* which is generally translated "non-self," "self-less," and "non-ego or egolessness." This book has opted for "interdependence."

Awareness: A transformative understanding based on Buddhist truths about the nature of reality and of the self. Not as complete as wisdom* or enlightenment.*

Birth-and-Death (*samsara*): (see transmigration*)

Bodhi: See enlightenment*.

Bodhisattvas: Awakened persons who devote their existence solely to leading others to the same awakened state or enlightenment (*bodhi*).

Buddha: An "awakened one" who is liberated from ignorance and thus one's suffering. Gotama or Shakyamuni is the most well-known Buddha and founder of Buddhism.

Buddha Lands (*buddha-kshetra* or *bukkoku* 仏国): Countless spiritual realms or pure lands* within the cosmos, each one presided over by a Buddha who hastens our enlightenment. Amida's *Sukhavati* is one such realm.

Buddhahood: the state or quality of a Buddha.

Buddha nature: The potential within all sentient beings to become Buddhas.

Dalai Lama: Title meaning "Teacher whose wisdom is as great as the ocean" and refers today to Tenzin Gyatso (1935–), the spiritual and political leader of the Tibetan people.

Dana: Voluntary and unconditional sharing of materials or wisdom with others. One of the Six Perfections*:

Dependent Co-arising (*pratitya-samutpada*): Doctrinal formula with twelve links (*nidanas*) that explains the chain of causes from ignorance to suffering; by eliminating ignorance, suffering is eliminated.

Dharma (*hō* 法): The fundamental spiritual truth that is the source of our enlightenment. It also refers to the teaching that leads us to enlightenment.

Dharmakara (Hōzō 法蔵): The name of the bodhisattva prior to becoming Amida* Buddha in the sacred story* that forms the centerpiece of the Larger Sutra*.

Eightfold Path: Set of practices that cultivates our mind and body for enlightenment. The fourth of the Four Noble Truths*.

Enlightenment (*bodhi*): Buddhahood* or the highest state of awareness, in which we realize our spiritual resolution. Attained by Shakyamuni Buddha* and countless Buddhists throughout history.

Four Marks of Existence: Basic principles that help us to awaken to truth by seeing life correctly. They are like corrective eyeglasses.

Four Noble Truths: A description in a nutshell of the Buddhist assumptions and practices: 1) suffering, 2) its cause, 3) its cessation and 4) the path.

Foolish being (*bombu* 凡夫): The true state of their own human condition painfully realized by those with Shinjin awareness*. They realize that they cannot liberate themselves through self-power*.

Honen: Shinran's teacher. The founder of the independent Pure Land movement in Japan and of the Jōdo School.

Hungry Ghosts: They suffer from constant unsatisfied hunger and occupy one of the six modes of existence: hell, hungry ghosts, beasts, titans, humans and heavenly beings.

Jōdo-Shinshū 浄土真宗: The Buddhist school founded by Shinran Sh]nin. It means "the true essence of the Pure Land way."

Karma: Actions of our mind, speech and body within the context of our spiritual cultivation. Does not mean fate.

Laypersons: Traditionally, the laypersons are made up of laymen (*upasakas*) and laywomen (*upasikas*), and they support the monks and nuns with materials.

Larger [Sukhavativyuha] Sutra: The most important of the three Jōdo-Shinshū canonical sutras because of its message of Amida's Primal Vow and Shinjin awareness.

Last Age of Dharma (*mappō* 末法): The third period in the history of declining quality of Buddhism and human life, preceded by the periods of True Dharma and Counterfeit Dharma.

Mahayana: "The Larger Vehicle" that refers to schools that emerged around the beginning of the Common Era with their new message that included a broader audience.

Meditation (*samadhi, dhyana, shamata*): Practice of realizing mental calm, control and clarity; one of the three elements of Three Training along with wisdom* and precepts.

Myōkōnin (妙好人): A category of deeply spiritual Jōdo-Shinshū persons likened to a rare White Lotus, recognized for their simple, selfless lives based on Shinjin*.

Name (*myōgō* 名号): The sacred name *Namo Amida Butsu* that embodies Amida* or Oneness*. We recite it on our own or together at temples as expression of deeply-felt gratitude.

Namo Amida Butsu (南無阿弥陀仏): A transliteration of the Sanskrit phrase, "I take refuge in the Buddha of Immeasurable [Light and Life]"; Shinran interpreted this phrase as embodying Amida itself. (see also *Name**)

Nembutsu (念仏): It originally meant to contemplate (*nem* 念) on the Buddha (*butsu* 仏), but in Jōdo-

Shinshū it means to recite the Name* as expression of profound gratitude.

Nirvana: The state of enlightenment* when greed, hatred and delusion have been completely "blown out." Persons in this state are none other than Buddhas (see enlightenment).

Oneness: (*dharmakaya* or *hosshin* 法身; *tathata* or *ichi'nyo* 一如): The ultimate source of spiritual awakening which is beyond ordinary conception. Through Amida* we experience its caring and interdependent nature. Comparative scholars often use "God-head."

Other Power (*tariki* 他力): The spiritual caring that we experience as the working of Amida's Primal Vow,* when we abandon self-power* practices or attempts to totally control our lives.

Primal Vow (*purva-pranidhana* or *hongan* 本願):In the sacred story* Amida raises forty-eight (the 18th being paramount) Bodhisattva* vows as expression of wish and prayer for all beings to be enlightened.

Pure Land (*Jōdo* 浄土): (See Buddha Land.*)

Pure Land Buddhism: A branch of the Mahayana movement that stressed compassion by offering a promise of Buddhahood to anyone upon birth in the Pure Land* of Amitabha (Amida*).

Rebirth: (see transmigration*)

Reincarnation: (see transmigration*)

Sacred Story: Refers to the *Larger Sutra** narrative of Bodhisattva* Dharmakara's process of becoming Amida Buddha in order to lead all beings to become Buddhas themselves.

Sangha: Community of monks, nuns and lay Buddhists. It constitutes one of the Three Treasures* along with Buddha* and Dharma*.

Satori (悟): A word that expresses enlightenment* especially in the Zen* tradition.

Self-power (*jiriki* 自力): Efforts to attain enlightenment* through one's own power or abilities without acknowledging or relying upon Other Power.*

Sentient Beings: All living creatures, not just humans, which possess potentials of becoming Buddhas.

Shakyamuni Buddha: (see Buddha*.)

Shinjin awareness (信心): The Jōdo-Shinshū transformative experience in this very life.

Shinran Shōnin (親鸞聖人): The founder of the Jōdo-Shinshū school.

Six Perfections (*paramita*): The well-known bodhisattva* practices: dana*, precepts, patience, vigor, meditation* and wisdom*.

Stage of Non-Retrogression (*futaiten-i* 不退転): (Essentially the same as the Stage of Truly Settled*.)

Stage of Truly Settled (*shōjō-ju* 正定聚): The state of joining a group of seekers who are assured of attaining Buddhahood immediately upon death as one of the benefits of Shinjin awareness*.

Sutra: The discourses that elucidate the Dharma, in most cases, by Shakyamuni Buddha.

Teachings: Shinran's main writing, *Kyōgyōshinshō*, a collection of passages from respected Mahayana* and Pure Land Buddhist* scriptures intended to refute criticisms of Honen's Pure Land teachings.

Tannishō: *Essay Lamenting Differences* was written by one of Shinran's disciples (perhaps Yui'en) to clarify his master's teachings; the most widely read Jōdo-Shinshū text today.

Theravada: "Teaching of the Elders," the dominant school of Buddhism in Sri Lanka and Southeast Asia. The only school today which does not belong to the Mahayana*.

Three Poisons: Greed, hatred and ignorance or delusions that obstruct us from realizing Buddhahood.

Three Treasures/Jewels: The Buddha*, Dharma* and Sangha*, which constitute our ideal, guide, and model. Taking refuge in them is the common ceremonial feature in all schools.

Transmigration: The cycle of birth-and-death (*samsara*) through the six modes of existence (See Hungry Ghosts) depending on one's karma*; Buddhist goal is to get off this cycle.

Wisdom (*prajna* or *chi'e* 智慧): Complete insight into the true nature of reality. Made possible by cultivating precepts and meditation.

Zen/Son/Ch'an: A meditative school of Buddhism in East Asia, whose Japanese form was made popular in the West initially through the writings of D.T. Suzuki.

Ocean

Suggested Further Readings:
Jodo-Shinshu Bibliography

A. Introductory – General Buddhism:

Rahula, Walpola. *What the Buddha Taught.* New York: Grove Weidenfeld, 1959. 151 pp. By far the best introduction in English to the basic Buddhist teachings. Utilizes the framework of the Four Noble Truths to discuss such crucial doctrines as *dukkha* (pain, suffering), nirvana, *anatta* (non-ego), and Eightfold Path.

Robinson, Richard H. *The Buddhist Religion: A Historical Introduction.* Belmont, California: Wadsworth Publishing Co., 1982. 290 pp. A thorough overview of basic doctrine and historical development of the various schools of Buddhism.

B. Introductory – Jodo-Shinshu

Dept. of Buddhist Education ed. *Shin Buddhist Service Book.* San Francisco: Buddhist Churches of America, 1994. 319 pp. Offers a glimpse into what

Jodo-Shinshu Buddhists do during the religious services. The service section covers the order of services, passages that are recited, sutras that are chanted and etiquette. The gatha section includes approximately 50 songs divided into English, Japanese and songs for special services, organ music and choral music.

Hisatsune, Kimi Yonemura. *Shinshu in Modern Society.* San Francisco: 1990. Reprint. Buddhist Churches of America, Dept. of Buddhist Education, 1995. 84 pp. A collection of essays by a thoughtful and perceptive woman writer on a wide range of contemporary topics as they pertain to Buddhism and Shinshu.

Jishin kyonin shin (Dharma School Teaching Guide). San Francisco: Buddhist Churches of America, 1987–88. A valuable set of teaching information for four grade levels: preschool, primary grades (1–3), intermediate (4–6), and advanced (7–8). A teaching guidebook and a workbook are available for each grade level. A rich resource that contains materials reflecting a long tradition of teaching Dharma to children in the English language.

Kodani, Masao. *Cocktails.* Los Angeles: Senshin Temple, 1992. 108 pp. Its preface starts out, "This booklet is a collection of terms, bits of information and historical facts — cocktail facts that might be of interest to Japanese-American Buddhists and Jodo-Shinshu Buddhists in particular who have often heard these terms but were never quite sure what they meant in English." An informative and handy reference for anyone interested in Jodo-Shinshu.

Kodani, Masao and Russell Hamada. *Traditions of Jodo-Shinshu Hongwanji-ha*. Los Angeles: Senshin Buddhist Temple, 1982. 124 pp. An excellent reference source on the ritual dimensions of the traditions: physical setting of the temples, robes and religious articles, basic rituals, holidays and festivals, rites of passages, chanting, family altar, honoraria, etc.

Kubose, Gyomay M. *Everyday Suchness*. Chicago: The Dharma House, 1967. 142 pp. This book by a pioneer minister from Chicago has become a "classic" especially for beginners with emphasis on the experiential rather than the doctrinal. Explains basic Buddhist concepts simply and addresses topics of popular interest in a down-to-earth manner. His second book, *The Center Within*, is also recommended.

Matsueda, Tsukasa. *From Iron Chain to Golden Chain: Dharma High School Readings*. San Francisco: Buddhist Churches of America, 1993. A collection of essays primarily by the author with contributions by a number of ministers. The *Iron Chain* is a reference to the World War II relocation experience of the Buddhists, while the Golden Chain points to the popular recitation at Jodo-Shinshu services. Written in a socio-historic framework, the book explores religious and sociological issues aimed at a high school level reading audience.

Ohtani, Yoshiko. *The Life of Eshinni: Wife of Shinran Shonin*. Translated by Taitetsu Unno. Kyoto: Jodo Shinshu Honganji-ha, 1990. 114 pp. Written by the wife of the 23rd Honganji Abbot Kosho Otani, the book contains an essay on Eshinni's life as seen from the author's pilgrimage experience and a translation of Eshinni's ten letters discovered in 1921 that greatly increased our understanding of Shinran's life.

Shin Buddhist Handbook. San Francisco: Buddhist Churches of America, 1972. 135 pp. Perhaps the best introductory overview of the teaching, history and practice for American/Western Jodo-Shinshu Buddhist readers. It includes a very helpful section on questions and answers, followed by sections devoted to services/rituals and practices. Well written and organized. Though it is now out of print, there are still enough copies in circulation. This should be revised and reprinted.

Tabrah, Ruth M. *The Monk Who Dared: An Historical Novel About Shinran*. Kailua, Hawaii: Press Pacifica, Ltd., 1994. 329 pp. Through her extensive research and imaginative portrayal, the author succeeds in filling in the hazy historical gaps and makes Shinran's first half of his life (monastery, tutelage under Honen, exile and marriage) come alive. This dramatic historical novel is the first by a woman and a Westerner about Shinran.

The Unbroken Promise. San Francisco: B.C.A., 1988. 29 pp. A collection of poems by followers and friends of Jodo-Shinshu Buddhists in North America, helping to open up to a living spiritual reality that cannot be adequately captured in ordinary language.

Yoshiyama, Katsumi Rev. *Simply Jodo Shinshu*. Trans. and published by Northwest Ministers' Association, 1994. 108 pp. A collection of 51 short sermon-style essays on a broad range of Shinshu topics from "The Land of Brightness" to "[Daily] Service."

C. More Advanced – Jodo-Shinshu

Bloom, Alfred. *Life of Shinran Shonin: The Journey to Self-Acceptance*. 1968. Reprint. Berkeley: Institute of Buddhist Studies, 1994. 80 pp. One of the earliest treatment of Shinran's life in English by a Western scholar. Scholastic in nature but this monograph can be enjoyed by non-specialists. The author raises many intriguing questions, for example, 1) why did Shinran enter the monastery, 2) why did he leave, 3) what were the specific charges against him, and 4) what prompted his return to Kyoto.

Bloom, Alfred. *Shinran's Gospel of Pure Grace*. Tucson: The Univ. of Arizona Press, 1965. 95 pp. The first systematic and "theological" treatment on Shinran by a Western scholar. Extremely popular in college classrooms and still in print after thirty years.

Bloom, Alfred. *Tannisho: Resource for Modern Living*. Honolulu: The Buddhist Study Center, 1981. 102 pp. Explains the most important chapters that illumine the heart of Shinshu teaching from the perspective of modern issues and concerns. Recently it was republished as *Strategies for Modern Living* by the Numata Center for Buddhist Research and Translation with a new translation of the *Tannisho*.

Bloom, Alfred. *Shoshinge: The Heart of Shin Buddhism*. Hawaii: Buddhist Study Center Press, 1986. 107 pp. A commentary on the set of poetic verses expressing Shinran's indebtedness to his spiritual masters and one which has played a central role in the Shinshu liturgical tradition; contains an English translation of the verses by T. Nagatani and R. Tabrah.

Dobbins, James C. *Jodo Shinshu: Shin Buddhism in Medieval Japan.* Bloomington and Indianapolis: Indiana University Press, 1989. 242 pp. An excellent historical treatment of the development of Shinshu institutions from Shinran to Rennyo. This book, in particular, fills "gaps" in previous scholarship in two areas: 1) contributions of Kaku'nyo (third abbot) and his son Zonkaku and 2) developments of the other Shinshu branches. The discussion of doctrinal heresy offers an innovative and insightful approach to our understanding of doctrine and its historical evolution.

Fujimoto, Ryukyo. *Shin Buddhism's Essence: The Tannisho* — Prof. Ryukyo Fujimoto's Translation, with Extracts from His Writings as Commentary. Edited by Tetsuo Unno. Los Angeles: Prof. Ryukyo Fujimoto Memorial Publication Ad Hoc Committee, 1993. 148 pp. Contains the author's translation of The Tannisho and a collection of brief essays on Shinshu doctrinal and historical topics. The book provides a glimpse into a respected scholar and teacher who inspired many of the Shinshu teachers in North America.

Keel, Hee Sung. *Understanding Shinran: A Dialogical Approach*. Fremont, Calif.: Asian Humanities Press, 1995. 210 pp. A work by a Korean Christian theologian that attempts to strike a more meaningful dialogue with Jodo-Shinshu. He questions the approach taken by modern scholars (e.g., *Shinran* by Ueda and Hirota) in presenting Shinran's thought and raises a number of issues which traditional treatments fail to see or dare to raise.

Kikumura, Norihiko. *Shinran: His Life and Thought*. Los Angeles: The Nembutsu Press, 1972. 192 pp. A concise book that introduces Shinran through the main phases of his life. It critically examines the scholarly theories surrounding the areas of controversy.

Kiyozawa, Manshi. *December Fan*: The Buddhist Essays of Manshi Kiyozawa. Trans. and ed. by Nobuo Haneda. Komiyama Printing Co., 98 pp. Kiyozawa (1863–1903) is one of the most pivotal Buddhist leaders in modern Jodo-Shinshu history. Belonging to the Higashi Honganji branch, this progressive priest helped to reform the teachings with message that resonated with modern Japan. Nobuo Haneda has translated other works by teachers of the Higashi branch, notably those of Maida Shuichi (1906–1967), in *Heard by Me* and *The Evil Person*.

Rogers, Minor L. and Ann T. Rogers. *Rennyo: The Second Founder of Shin Buddhism*. Berkeley, California: Asian Humanities Press, 1991. 434 pp. A thorough study of the eighth abbot (monshu) of the Hongwanji branch, Rennyo (1415–1499), with a translation of his letters and a discussion and analysis of his life and his preeminent role in the development of the largest Jodo-Shinshu institution.

Ueda, Yoshifumi and Dennis Hirota. *Shinran: An Introduction to His Thought*. Kyoto: Hongwanji Int. Center, 1989. 372 pp. The most comprehensive and systematic presentation so far of Shinran's thought in a single volume. It places Shinran within the development of Mahayana Buddhist thought. It contains ample translations of key passages from his writings based on major doctrinal themes. Authored by two main translators of the Shin Buddhist Translation Series.

Yamaoka, Seigen. *True Pure Land Buddhism: Jodoshinshu: An Introduction*. Los Angeles: Pure Land Publications, 1991. 65 pp. Provides a good traditional overview of the major doctrines, supported by appropriate citations from the original sources. Written from within the tradition with emphasis on orthodox doctrine. May prove to be difficult reading for those looking for spiritual edification on an introductory level.

Translations of Jodo-Shinshu scriptures

Inagaki, Hisao. *The Three Pure Land Sutras*. Kyoto: Nagata Bunshodo, 1994. 465 pp. A modern, readable translation in one volume of the three canonical Jodo-Shinshu sutras: *The Larger Sutra, The Contemplation Sutra* and *The Smaller Sutra*. Also contains approximately 200 pages devoted to an overview of major doctrine and of eminent Pure Land Buddhist figures and their doctrinal contributions.

Shin Buddhist Translation Series: Since 1978 a team of scholars sponsored by the Hongwanji International Center in Kyoto has successfully translated the major works of Shinran:

Letters of Shinran (*Mattosho*), 1978
Notes on 'Essentials of Faith Alone' (*Yuishinsho mon'i*), 1979
Notes on Once-calling and Many-calling (*Ichinen-tanen mon'i*), 1980
Notes on the Inscriptions on Sacred Scrolls (*Songo shinzo meimon*), 1981
Passages on the Pure Land Way (*Jodo monrui jusho*), 1982
The True Teachings, Practice and Realization of the Pure Land Way (*Kyogyoshinsho*). (Referred to as *The Teachings* in the book):

Volume I, *Chapters on Teaching and Practice*, 1983
Volume II, *Chapter on Shinjin*, 1985
Volume III, *Chapters on Realization and True Buddha and Land*, 1987
Volume IV, *Chapter on Transformed Buddha-Bodies and Lands*, 1990

<u>Hymns of the Pure Land</u> (*Jodo wasan*), 1991
<u>Hymns of the Pure Land Masters</u> (*Koso wasan*), 1992
<u>Hymns of the Right, Semblance, and Last Dharma-Ages</u> (*Shozomatsu wasan*), 1993

Unno, Taitetsu, trans. *Tannisho: A Shin Buddhist Classic*. Honolulu: Buddhist Study Center Press, 1984. 73 pp. An easy to read translation of perhaps the most popular Shinshu book due to its direct and simple way of expressing the heart of Shinshu spirituality. This book is recommended for its glossary of key Shinshu terms, concise explanation of basic concepts and an excellent bibliography for studies.

Ocean

Index A

Questions Most Often Asked

Jodo-Shinshu Buddhism

Index B